Christians
with
Secular Power

Laity Exchange Books
Mark Gibbs, General Editor

Called to Holy Worldliness
by Richard J. Mouw

Christians with Secular Power

Mark Gibbs

FORTRESS PRESS   **Philadelphia**

LAITY EXCHANGE BOOKS

To
My Friends and Colleagues at Vesper Society

Library of Congress Cataloging in Publication Data

Gibbs, Mark.
   Christians with secular power.

   (Laity exchange books)
   Bibliography: p.
   1. Laity. I. Title. II. Series.
   BV687.G48   248.4   80–8048
   ISBN 0–8006–1389–9

8292G80   Printed in the United States of America   1–1389

Contents

Preface

THIS SERIES of *Laity Exchange Books* is intended to stimulate the Christian laity in the exercise of their ministry today, particularly in the secular world outside church walls and organizations. In the planning of the series, it has been clear that one of the most difficult topics on which to find any helpful material is that kind of Christian obedience and discipleship appropriate for Christians in positions of power and responsibility. There are many useful books on lay ministries in church work and committees, a good many on personal and caring ministries in local neighborhoods and in voluntary organizations, and not a few on involvement in radical causes and movements; but there is much less available to help either laity or clergy think through some of the hard questions of lay involvement in the secular structures of today's world. Indeed in recent years some church trainers and enablers have seemed to consider such secularly involved laity either as helpless zombies fatally entangled in corrupting and demonic "powers" and structures, or else as hypocritical Christians paying lip service to the gospel on Sundays and in their domestic lives but cheerfully exploiting their fellow men and women every Monday morning. I am absolutely convinced that many lay people may find a true ministry in their lives as politicians, business executives, or union leaders. Hence this book, which may at least start off some Christian discussions and even controversies.

I am particularly conscious of the debt I owe to the large number of people who have helped and encouraged me. I am extremely grateful to Jack Collins of the National Council of Churches and to James Baird, Jr., of the United Presbyterian Church, who in 1974 arranged a study grant which produced not only a series of articles on the European academies and laity centers but also some of the ideas and first drafts for this book.

Robert P. Brorby made some sharp and much appreciated criticism of the first draft of chapter 1, and at the same time persistently encouraged me in the whole project. My dear colleague, the late Dr. T. Ralph Morton, helped a great deal with chapter 2, even though this was, sadly, one of the rare occasions on which we disagreed on the line to be taken. Many of my colleagues on the Audenshaw Project and on the Christian Frontier Council, London, helped with earlier drafts of chapters 2 and 3 (part of the latter chapter was published in *Audenshaw Papers* no. 51). Chapter 4 benefited particularly from discussions with Arthur Walmsley and Ted Eastman. Chapter 5 owes much to comments from Tom Matheny and to discussions with friends in the European laity centers, especially Paul-Gerhard Seiz and Martin Stäbler of Bad Boll; in chapters 5 and 7 some material comes from Frontier Council discussions and various reports in *Audenshaw Documents* no. 19 and *Audenshaw Papers* no. 37. Monsignor George Higgins was both gracious and speedy in helping me with some sources in chapter 8.

I cannot mention everybody, for people have been very generous with information and criticism. But I cannot forbear to list Arild and Elise Olsen, Charity Waymouth, Barry Menuez, Cynthia Wedel, Harry Morton, Francis and Margaret House, Michael and Adèle Taylor, and Mels and Cecily Chalmers for their special support and encouragement. I am also deeply grateful to Marjorie Figures, Jean Cole, and Connie Brunskill who have typed and retyped much of the manuscript.

MARK GIBBS

PART ONE

PROBLEMS OF RESPONSIBILITY

1

A Common Calling: Some Special Responsibilities

> Grant that they may both perceive and know what things they ought to do, and also may have grace and power faithfully to fulfill the same.
>
> The Collect for the First
> Sunday after Epiphany

> Laymen and women are not merely to be instructed in theology, but are often the principal agents in discerning and responding to the Spirit of God.
>
> A report at the Christian Conference
> of Asia, June 1973

THIS BOOK is primarily for those Christians who wield secular power and for those—laity or clergy—who wish to understand and to support the ministries of their powerful fellow believers. Nevertheless, before we can move to examine the special responsibilities of such people, I believe that it is essential for us to review and to emphasize what the gospel proclaims about God's wonderful calling to all human beings on the face of the earth—powerful and powerless alike. I make no apology for repeating here some familiar themes in Christian theology, and in particular familiar themes in what has been called the "theology of the laity," for these are central to our understanding of the mission of the whole

3

people of God.[1] These themes can—even in the darkest days—
supply a Christian vision for the future, and find a way to illuminate
the vocation not only of powerful people but of everybody else as
well.

Can we sound such a certain note, in the last quarter of the
twentieth century, after so many interminable controversies about
our theological understanding of Christian beliefs? Can we now
assert that intelligent, critical, secularly minded laity can find any
clear understanding of what it means to be a follower of Jesus
Christ in our modern, skeptical, technologically dominated society? Yes, I believe we can. Despite all our contemporary confusions (not so new, if you look at past centuries of religious history) I
maintain that the church as a whole does have some reasonable and
challenging ideas about the kind of laity we may hope to be—
people with a certain kind of Christian faith, people with a certain
way of Christian living.

On matters of faith we might as well admit from the start that
many lay people have tended to believe rather less than what their
official churches and clergy have urged them to subscribe to. This
particular skepticism, was echoed, for instance, by T. S. Eliot,
"They seem so certain of what they believe. My own beliefs are
held with a scepticism which I never even hope to be quite rid of."[2]
Such frankness helps a good deal now that so many of the credal
statements of earlier centuries are in question. But such a sincere
and entirely desirable "agnosticism" about many past Christian
beliefs and even superstitions does not rule out a strong and life-
dominating belief in certain basic essentials, certain core truths
about God and the world as revealed to us by Jesus Christ. (If
professional theologians no longer subscribe in any sense at all to
these core truths, then they—if not we—are in trouble.)

Some Central Beliefs

1. We see through a glass darkly (especially if the glass has not
been cleaned for a long time), but we *can* see something. Our vision
is imperfect, partial, blurred, but it is not completely false. God has
shown and does show us something of himself and his purposes for
us—most especially in the records of the life and teaching of Jesus

Christ, in the records of the early Christians, and in the records of the development of the church. It is most important to emphasize that this is the story of the development of the *whole* church—not just the clergy and official teachers, but the laity as well; not just Baptists or Episcopalians or Methodists but all the people of God, from Quakers to Roman Catholics and back again, and including many people a bit outside the traditional and sober structures of our ecclesiastical organizations; not just the sometimes glorious, sometimes hideous, and sometimes dusty church history of past centuries but the church in recent years and *now*. (Why does official church history concentrate so much on ecclesiastical matters? Why does it so often leave out the laity? Why does it so often stop with David Livingstone or Dietrich Bonhoeffer?)

It is no doubt unfair, but God does not tell the English everything, nor American Lutherans, nor Italian Roman Catholics. *One way or another, if we seek, we shall find.*

2. God as revealed in Jesus Christ is generous, not grudging. Certainly he expects us to face up to sin and failure, but he forgives, if necessary time and again, and we can live by his graciousness, not by our little achievements or miseries. This doctrine of salvation by grace is tremendously important for laity immersed in murky, confusing, compromising situations: it is truly liberating for them. God's Holy Spirit is for them, too, as it is for all of us. I remember a prayer used by President James McCord of Princeton Seminary: "The past is forgiven, the future is open." That gives both comfort and strength.

3. God offers us the chance of being part of his new creation *now*, of being citizens of his new kingdom *now*—not just after death. The strongest laity are those who know that they have two citizenships, two nationalities, all the time. This is the key to the right kind of Christian patriotism, and it transforms much of the present uneasiness about death and dying.

4. The strongest laity are also those who know, and are determined to cling to, their ministries in the secular world of today and tomorrow. They know this instinctively, even if they can't express it theologically. They really are committed to be friends, counselors, ministers, and priests not only to their own family and

friends, but also in their neighborhood and their place of work. They ache to relate their Christian faith to the power struggles and opportunities and corruptions of the structures of government and industry. They have some Christian hope left, and more than a faint vision of truly human structures and societies for tomorrow and the day after tomorrow. They are not utopians, but they resist, somehow, the temptation to wallow in gloom and to join in the nostalgia for the good old days for the middle class. At the same time they resist the interminable pressures (largely from clergy, who ought to know better) to overemphasize the importance of church structures, and to pretend that it is more Christian to be on a church committee than on a community school board. They refuse to be entangled too much in church housekeeping and organization (though, notwithstanding, they often do more than their share of this work), for they know their calling is to be faithful in the structures of the world.

Always Learning

The impressive thing about the most effective laity that I meet is their capacity to learn, their *habit* of learning all kinds of things in all kinds of ways. They have known, long before the jargon became fashionable, how to combine intellectual and affective learning, how to develop their emotions, their imagination, their sexuality, without falling for the sloppy antiintellectualism of our times. They have learned how to develop a deep love for their family and for friends (develop it, not pretend to instant intimacy), how to meet openly and courteously all kinds of people they come up against, and how to burn, yes, burn for justice for millions of their fellow human beings whom they will never know personally at all.

This is, of course, what makes for really effective adult living in the modern world; but for the Christian laity there are two things more: a constant attempt to assess the new knowledge, the new experience, the new challenge, against what has been called "the mind of Christ," the vision which we have—imperfect yet genuine—of what God wants for us and for his world; and a readiness to be thoroughly obedient to what we learn. The best laity know how to "accept and work for change" and know something of the real costs of that glib phrase in both personal and family, and work and political situations. They do take risks, they do stay flexible and resilient, they do work extra hard in new ways and on new problems. They develop a kind of Christian and (as the Germans call it) "civil" courage.

Such laity are people who enjoy the world, as they can. They say a definite yes to many of the blessings of the twentieth century (even automobiles), and they hope that such comforts may be shared by more and more people. They know all about the dangers of affluence; they enjoy the world, but they are not enslaved by it; and they hope to be ready for bad times when they come. Even if they are young, they know and accept something of the tragedy of human life, for like Lady Mary Montagu "they came young into the hurry of the world," and they do not pretend that pain and sickness and loneliness and messy terminal illnesses are always avoidable. They know, too, that there may be bitter job and financial insecurities these days (even for the whitest-collared workers), that personal relationships are not achieved automatically or easily, and that there may be treacheries or sexual miseries, as there always have been. Yet such laity are strong; they have endurance; sometimes they have serenity. They have a depth of Christian experience which makes much of the blather about "joyful, meaningful relationships" seem pitifully shallow. And they are, mostly, very busy people—and not ashamed of this. There is a great deal to be done, and if one is to be responsible about one's family, one's job, one's politics and one's church, and at the same time enjoy life, offer hospitality, and not be a dour spoilsport, then one will be busy. But they strive also for times of quiet, for reflection and prayer, and some kind of worship. They mean to be busy, but they know well enough the dangers of overbusyness.

This marvelous calling to be neither sheep nor children but strong, adult, Christian disciples is for *all* people. It is tragic and almost demonic that such a glorious equality of vocation has constantly been narrowed down and twisted by church teachers, so that some kind of hierarchy, some kind of Byzantine or medieval or Victorian class system has made "all called, but some more called than others." Clergy are more called than laity, Protestants more than Catholics, rich more than poor, landowners more than peasants, Westerners more than natives, whites more than blacks, university graduates more than illiterates, bankers more than blue-collar workers, men far more than women. There are so many background assumptions of this kind—psychological hang-ups as well as sub-Christian doctrines—that, as Dr. Barbara Zikmund has written, there is often "an insidious double standard which speaks of clergy having a call to the ministry and other people getting a job."[3] It is disgraceful how some churches have distorted the word *vocation* to mean only a clerical or churchly work, as in the old tag, "I have a vocation, you have an occupation, he has a job." There are equally insidious assumptions which rank working-for-people careers as worthy but the occupations of politicians and business people as hardly legitimate for "true" Christians.

In All Our Responsibilities

This calling is to *all* people, and for *all* of our lives. God's calling to us is not only to be faithful in our church membership, our family responsibilities and our personal relationships, our neighborly duties to those who live near us and maybe work with us, but also in our occupational responsibilities, whatever the job may be. This is primarily a matter of serving and relating the gospel to the structures of modern life in which we are involved, not just being pleasant and kind to fellow workers.

It is more than a matter of our work life. We also have to work out our Christian faith in our leisure time, which for Western people is becoming more and more the major interest of our lives—vacations, weekends, sports, entertainments, retirement years. Christian people have a bad record here of simply being spoilsports: I have never forgotten the passion with which a young man once said to me in Manchester, England, "For God's sake, keep God out of Saturday night!" Of course the Lord insists on being involved in Saturday night, just as much as in Sunday morning, but not, surely, in the censorious way which this student feared. We must develop a theology of leisure as well as a revised theology of work, especially in countries more and more affected by technological change, and moving toward a four-day week, at least a month's vacation each year, and often retirement at age fifty-five.

But still more—since God's calling is to put our entire lives at his disposal—we must include a proper stewardship of our political responsibilities. Many Christians still have a political theology suitable for fellow slaves in the Roman Empire, or peasants in a medieval village. We are called to live in a world which has seen something of a vision of fair, decent, and just democracies; rather than Christians despising their fellow believers who involve themselves deeply in political systems, they should honor and affirm and support them for the courage they show and the risks they take. This is discussed at greater length in chapters 2 and 6.

It is notorious that some narrow definitions of lay responsibilities have even restricted our calling to our church membership—to "turn up, sit up, pay up, and shut up" as the old saying has it. The almost equally damaging limitation of the Christian vocation to what has been called "the soft end of the spectrum"—the personal, loving, affectionate responsibilities to family, friends, and neighbors—has not been sufficiently appreciated, even in many Protestant churches which in theory affirm the "priesthood of all believers" and the calling of the laity. It cannot be said too often that God calls us not only to love, deeply and personally and lastingly, those whom we know face-to-face, but also to work for justice toward many world citizens whom we shall never know personally at all.

We are, then, all called to and privileged to enjoy a common vocation, to be part of the new humanity in Christ Jesus, men and women of a new quality of life. God has no favorites (that oft repeated message of the New Testament obscured by the quaint traditional translation "God is no respecter of persons"). He has no favorites, he loves us all; and that both destroys our constant temptations to spiritual pride and gives us all hope.

Nevertheless, there is a wonderful variety among the people of God. Despite the pressures to social conformity in many congregations, we are not expected to live identical lives, in identical jobs and homes. We are equal in our vocation; we are profoundly different and varied and unequal in our talents and interests. One of the passages in the New Testament which has been admirably opened up for the ordinary reader by modern translations is 1 Corinthians 12, in which Paul speaks of our different gifts and work, and how we should rejoice in their variety in the one great church. It is clear that we are to develop what talents and gifts we have, rather than all of us trying to be preachers, or doctors, or community workers.

We must now move to examine the special responsibilities of those Christians in positions of secular power, and we must try to avoid the confusions that Eugene Goodheart castigated when he complained about "that Christian and modern sentimentality that pretends that weakness is strength or that refuses to make distinctions among various orders of strength and weakness."[4]

The Kinds of Power

The phrase "secular power" needs some clarification, at least as it relates to the scope of this chapter. Power can be defined in many different ways, and phrases such as "spiritual power" or "the true power of powerlessness" can be used emotively and a little confusingly by many Christian people. We may begin to classify the different kinds of power in the modern world—whether or not they are recognized as proper for Christians to exercise—like this: military power, political power, economic power, intellectual power, psychological power, and spiritual power (though many would hesitate to make this a clear separate category apart from the others).

This book deals primarily with Christians concerned with military, political, and economic power, rather than with intellectual and psychological power. (There is surely need for another useful book on such matters.) It will maintain that the spiritual power of Christians is intimately related to their use of other kinds of power; it is not essentially a separate and special gift unrelated to the messiness of life.

In the past, Christians in government and in the corporations had perhaps too much attention given to them, at least in the United States. They were not quite at the top of the Christian totem pole—that was reserved for senior clergy—but they were given careful attention and their share of elegant memorials. In recent years, there has been an extreme reaction against such "establishment" Christians, who are accused of sitting far too comfortably in their privileged positions, and sometimes even of using religion as a cloak for maintaining a distinctly unfair political and economic system. The unthinking assumptions about the virtues of such laity in past generations have been replaced by equally unexamined assumptions about the lukewarm commitment of upper-middle-class Christians today. Indeed, such concepts as Christian leadership or dedicated ability are now highly suspect. As Andrew Morton of the British Council of Churches put it recently, "To be powerful—or even worse, to be happy about it—is indecent."[5]

Certainly we have every right to examine and criticize the work and the life-styles of those in positions of special responsibility. Certainly we need to probe very deeply into the assumptions they make, the privileges they claim, the traditions they wish to defend, the innovations they wish to encourage. The chapters that follow will not forget these questions. But at the outset I think we ought to acknowledge that the world has to be run, somehow. Except under conditions of terrible global disasters, such as a series of nuclear wars, humankind will not return to simple village life: indeed the inexorable advance of technology (no doubt now energy-conscious technology) seems to me one of the given facts of the twentieth century, whatever kind of political system we have, whatever shortages develop, whatever new riches are found. Both government and private industry are going to demand greater, not lesser strengths in leadership and management. Of course this will, we hope, be a more democratic, sensitive, fair style of leadership, but leadership it will be.

As Ralph Morton once wrote:

I increasingly dislike the word "leader" but it's hard to find another; and there are undeniable qualities that some people must have to do certain jobs. Competence is obviously important. But there's another necessary quality. And it's not abrasiveness. It might be called "vision." It's the power to see further into the future than others and the ability to awaken men's imaginations.[6]

It was Peter Berger who prophesied some years ago that if Harvard and Princeton graduates insisted on the "greening of America"—moving off to rural communes instead of going to jobs in Washington or Wall Street—then the "blueing of America" would follow: executive jobs would be filled by able recruits from blue-collar families, maybe less polished but eager to take the management and political jobs which have to be filled if a country of 200 million people is to function at all. We have many examples from twentieth-century history that if decent liberal-democratic governments fail to govern and to keep their countries running, fail to avoid economic chaos or massive inflation, then more autocratic systems will take their place. Edmund Burke was right: "For evil to triumph, it is only necessary for good men to do nothing." For unsatisfactory styles of government and of political and industrial leadership to develop in America, it is only necessary for Christian people—and other people of goodwill—to keep away from political and industrial jobs, and to forget to support, with their prayers and a sensitive as well as a critical understanding, those whom God has called to serve him in such difficult and responsible positions. The Christian church needs first and foremost to understand what it means to be a leader and to wield power, especially in the United States, where there are so many unfinished plans for social and economic reform, where the challenges to leadership are now so daunting, and the rewards, though often very substantial, may sometimes be described as "less money, more ulcers." The church needs to help young Christians to have the courage to take up such careers, and it needs to know how to support them and help them educate themselves through the tough struggles to top management or to senior political office. We must know how to encourage and to affirm them as well as when to criticize them. We must recognize, and show clearly that we recognize, that their commitment to Jesus Christ, even in the messy, muddled, ambiguous struggles of present-day politics and business, can be quite as acceptable to him as the dedicated lives of, say, suburban clergymen or community schoolteachers.

2

The Strains and the Compromises

Accept the strength. Put up with your share of difficulties.

2 Tim. 2:1–3

Those who lived in the time of Hitler and Stalin know that the worst is always possible; keeping faith means believing that it is not always certain.

RAYMOND ARON, *In Defense of Decadent Europe*

WE MAY HOPE to find Christian laity who are deeply involved in the structures of political and economic power and who are strong in their secular skills and in their Christian commitment to stay in those secular structures. However, if we examine their lives today in the 1980s, we soon find that many of them feel that the pressures on them are remarkably heavy. Their complaints are loud. This is generally true whether they are conservatives or reformers, Republicans or Democrats, whether they are in political office, in financial and banking leadership, or in industrial corporations. It is therefore important that we should examine why they feel under such strain, and without necessarily reinforcing popular Wall Street myths about the hard lives of corporation executives, we have some obligation to look sympathetically before we look critically at their present situation.

A life of real leadership has normally been rather strenuous, even in the comfortable upper-class styles of the eighteenth and nineteenth centuries. It is, however, apparent that in our century, even in the most conventional boardrooms and government agencies, the strains have increased perceptibly. Many corporation executives now face, as early as in their forties, serious pressures from their younger colleagues and competitors. Constant mergers and takeovers, even within what were formerly staid and established industries, extraordinary technological innovations in recent years, and sharp competition from growing industrial nations like South Korea, make for personal insecurity on a scale unusual in the past. (It is little comfort to executives to remind them that blue-collar workers have almost always suffered such insecurities.) Even career civil servants in Washington or London, who expect to enjoy job security and pension schemes even the archangels might envy, are by no means as sure as they used to be of a steady, pleasant promotion pattern.

None of this will sound particularly terrible to a family on relief, or to a storefront minister struggling to keep an old Volkswagen running while noticing the company Buicks on the freeways. Most upper-middle-class people in the United States—as in Britain— have no idea how lucky they are, even with present taxes and inflation. But if we are to understand the responsibilities of Christians in leadership positions, we have to recognize some of these personal worries and preoccupations, even if we have to ask them to shake themselves out of the self-pity of some of their colleagues.

It Is Worse These Days

We can list a number of special problems which have become more intense in the last few years.

There is a numbing feeling of helplessness among senior people in many executive positions, *which they can do almost nothing about,* because even quite large departments and companies are caught up in giant national and international structures—for example, corporations, unions, and political power blocs. It is not true that large-scale organizations are necessarily bad or inhuman (it is difficult to envisage a steel industry or a telephone company operating on the principle that small is beautiful); however, at the moment many production targets and many employment figures are at risk because of things out of the control of the executives. This is particularly frustrating for those who have already learned and experienced new styles of intelligent organizational change within their own firms or departments, and who intensely dislike firing colleagues and employees who have become redundant through no fault of their own.

There is a nagging background fear that sometimes those who are leaders, those who in theory have even more power and responsibility and who have to make the really giant decisions, that those people (often politicians) are not all that competent nor effectively in control. The extraordinary revelations about the Nixon administration, not only the corruption but also the capriciousness, and the stories and rumors about the uncertainties of the Carter style of government, have not reassured anybody.

Uncertainty exists about what acceptable styles of leadership and organization in modern politics and industry are. This is in some ways a very healthy anxiety; the extraordinarily persistent paternalism and the old assumptions about the rights of management really have to be questioned, not only in the bright new plants of IBM and Texas Instruments but in the industrial backwoods of New Jersey and New Hampshire. Such necessary criticism has, however, sometimes produced a sour caricature of management today, replicated again and again in popular magazines and church pamphlets. We owe a considerable debt to James McGregor Burns for emphasizing that, while sometimes political and business leaders may exercise transformational, charismatic leadership (the kind most easily recognized by religious people), much of the work of running the world has to be achieved by various forms of transactional leadership, in whch bargains have to be negotiated and compromises achieved.[1] This kind of leadership (in which Franklin Roosevelt and Lyndon Johnson excelled) is often suspect to Christians, although in fact most senior clergy and church executives have to practice similar skills much of the time.

Doomsday Depressions

There are a number of excessively gloomy social theories which infect, rather than inform, contemporary thinking about business and industry. Certainly the 1980s will be years of industrial difficulties, particularly with respect to energy supplies; but it is a rumor, not a proven fact, that "the west is doomed," that the present way of life from Japan to California to Britain to the Federal Republic of Germany is inevitably cracking up.

A second kind of half-unconscious disaster thinking is semi-Marxist in flavor. It consists of a vague feeling that capitalist society is collapsing, that inherent strains and class tensions will eventually break it up, and that anything we do only patches up an economic system predestined to die. It is strange that so many church people, both conservatives and liberals, half accept these defeatist and defensive attitudes, and yet do not face squarely and intelligently such social theories. Of course both Karl Marx's analysis of early capitalism and the various forms of developed Marxist theories propounded today deserve careful examination, but that is quite different from allowing what can only be called pseudo-Marxist superstitions to distract us from a realistic examination of whether our social systems are capable of renewal or not.

Personal Strains

In addition to the special strains which face leaders today, we must remember the familiar burdens on executives which have been recognized for many years. The difficulties of maintaining a rich and enjoyable family life despite frequent business engagements, have not lessened. The predilection of the young for alternative life-styles, denunciations of the "system," and at least as much unorthodox sex, drugs, and drink as in past generations have not diminished parental anxieties in affluent homes. Some executives remain remarkably healthy, but the long hours, the fogbound airports, the tastelessly expensive hotels, the mountains of paper, the dreary committees (especially in government work) are a great weariness to the flesh and spirit and produce a stale tiredness which can poison personal relationships at home, at work, and in the congregation.

The Temptation to Withdraw

Indeed it is no wonder that many able executives long for the day when they may cultivate their gardens. There is a special danger that the most scrupulous people, the most sensitive, may too easily choose to withdraw from the heat of battle, the tensions of the hard bargaining, and the messy bargains of elections. They become consultants or assistants in various kinds of nonprofit social or church work (admirable activities in themselves) and so leave secular power to the more ruthless. Other political and industrial leaders are greatly tempted to withdraw into a kind of cynical defensiveness, a private world of comfortable homes, country clubs, and exclusive vacations which can become a reassuring separate milieu for them and their friends. But this does not integrate them into the life of the nation or of the church. Indeed, such attitudes may well be part of the gentle corruption which wealth may bring, even to sincere Christians.

I believe that there is really only one great Christian doctrine which can support lay people deeply involved in such secular problems and beset by such concerns. We noted it in the last chapter; it is relevant to all the lives of all God's people, but it has particular strength for laity in positions of power and responsibility. It is, of course, the doctrine of God's grace—his graciousness and marvelous willingness to forgive, to strengthen, to accept ordinary, sinful, bewildered, depressed men and women as his partners in the fashioning of a new humanity. I find that surprising numbers of lay people active in secular power structures are still haunted by the superstition that God is fundamentally a rather grudging inspector of souls reluctantly accepting us as "saved" if we can show a reasonable tally of good deeds and donations, and a not too bad record of petty sins and faults (thought of as mostly sexual). If only we can understand, if only the clergy taught us more about, the incredible *eagerness* of God, as shown by Jesus Christ, to bless us, to help us, to put our lives straight, to lead us through the dangerous jobs and murky political swamps and give us courage for the tough and messy business of modern living. This is his grace, his loving generosity. It has nothing to do with either our modest achievements or our dreary months of underachieving anything worthwhile.

And especially, if we could only understand the eagerness of God to give us courage. All honor to many young people who decide for right and proper reasons that God does not call them to careers in the secular structures of society, but I suspect that a *wrong* reason why some church people may go into safe and recognizably good serving and caring jobs is that they feel becoming a nurse or a teacher (or still more, an ordained minister) is bound to be more worthwhile, and less dangerous to the soul and the personality, than a job which involves wielding power and bargaining in the marketplace, allocating cash jobs, and hiring and firing people. We need to insist that such an attitude may be timid and overcautious. It may be selfish and sinful. It may reflect a deep-down feeling that purity of our souls is what matters, and that such purity may be best achieved by keeping out of difficult jobs and situations. There are several warnings from our Lord that "he who seeketh his soul shall lose it"; I think these warnings apply to some who shun compromising situations in private or in public life. We need to take seriously the blunt comment of Saul Alinsky: "He who sacrifices the mass good for his personal salvation has a peculiar conception of 'personal salvation': he doesn't care enough for people to be 'corrupted' for them."[2]

The Necessity for Responsible Compromises

There, now, is the difficult and unpleasant word: compromise. It has become a word with almost entirely bad meanings in the English language. Every time there is a national scandal over corruption, every time there is talk of a settlement in Zimbabwe-Rhodesia or in the Middle East, earnest preachers—secular or religious—urge us "not to compromise," not to "live by an adjusted conscience," not to "let Jesus down" by bargaining for less than the best. Sometimes they are entirely right, but not always. The tensions inherent in the exercise of power are not always frankly faced by contemporary theologians—particularly when they are writing for the laity. Reinhold Niebuhr and Helmut Thielicke have been shining exceptions here.[3]

Not many have spoken as clearly as the English layman Philip Mason when he wrote:

At every turn, professing Christians are up against some form of the same dilemma. We proclaim the Word made Flesh, the Light that came into the world—and, in that Light, the thought of compromise is horrible. We want to reject any obedience less than perfect. Yet in practice, human society is based on compromise. Politics is always a compromise between different interests.[4]

It is time that more church people realized and openly accepted the fact that all political, industrial, commercial, and public life is a matter of exercising power, and that almost all effective use of power is a matter of endless bargaining and compromise solutions, many of them entirely honorable ones. We must work out, again and again, the responsible compromises which have to be accepted in order to avoid irresponsible, unacceptable compromises.

In fact, we must recognize that keeping out of the murky situations of public life by escaping into the so-called morally safe jobs or by retreating to a happy Californian commune *is in itself a compromise,* not a "pure" stance of Christian love. For some it may be the right compromise, gaining something in Christian living and service, but forgoing other opportunities for Christian living and service. Again, a move to any stance of total revolution, of radical reform, of an attempt to turn a country or an economy into a completely new society, is also a compromise. Some Christians in such situations may feel it right to be revolutionaries, but again they have to assess under God the gains and the losses of such a stance, whether they adopt violent or nonviolent styles of revolution.

We need to understand that the worst compromises are often those into which people slide without realizing what is happening, those in which people get caught because they are too lazy, or too fearful, to know what is happening. A wise young student of mine said once, when faced with the moral perplexities of Lancashire business life, "The main thing is to know what is going on." An intelligent perception of the shifts in power and of the strengths and weaknesses of colleagues, will often enable a Christian executive to anticipate difficult situations, and to be ready for them.

We must also accept the fact that younger, junior leaders are relatively unfree people in many industrial and political structures. If they are to achieve any real power and do any real good, then there is a promotion ladder to be climbed, and political and business bosses to be watched. Sometimes, of course, it may be right to protest, despite the horrible results for them and their families' fortunes; sometimes, wisely, their seniors will encourage them to speak their mind and show that they do not require a subservient acquiescence. Earnest young recruits who lodge a moral protest once a week, however, do not often achieve real seniority and power, even in the most liberal establishments. In Victorian England the young Mr. Gladstone was lucky that Lord Palmerston, his prime minister, dealt rather amiably with his frequent offers of resignation on matters of conscience, but Mr. Gladstone was fortunate enough to have an independent income and influential patrons. In any case he had to learn how to survive in nineteenth-century English politics, how to win elections, how to struggle with the miserable complexities of the Irish question, and how to exercise great power at a time when Britain was really powerful. On the whole, it is evident that by a series of wise and responsible compromises, Mr. Gladstone did great good. Similar opportunities and similarly ambiguous situations face any political leader in Washington or Sacramento today.

Such a catalog of difficulties makes rather a formidable and depressing list. We must remember the point in the last chapter; there are, in spite of these difficulties, many convinced Christian laity of high quality in and around the American churches today, neither miserable nor overwhelmed by the political and economic confusions of recent months. Yes, there are strains, but in one way or another they have achieved considerable skill in coping with them, whether they face personal and family worries, the convolutions of Washington's energy policies, or the problems of exporting to the Middle East. What such strong laity often lack, and often know that they lack, is a theological understanding of their vocation under God, and how this applies to their occupations and their public responsibilities. How the churches may help them to be theologically strong, as they are already professionally and personally strong, is a topic we return to in the second part of this book. But first we must consider the position of Christians in situations of much more severe difficulty.

3

Under Brutal Strain

> It is your duty to know, and to be haunted by your knowledge.
>
> ARTHUR KOESTLER

> Remember those that are in bonds.
>
> Heb. 13:3

For many of our fellow world citizens this is a century of repression and torture, not a century of freedom. Since World War I so many beastly and tyrannical political regimes have been established that large numbers of Christian people have lived under conditions of harsh political restrictions, and many Christians exercising responsibilities in state or business structures have again and again been faced with quite hideous moral compromises. They are under appalling pressure to conform. Certainly, in some parts of our modern world, there are now new hopes of achieving both personal freedom and economic and social justice (the news from Spain, Portugal, and Greece has been heartening), but for many of the people of God it is not normal to live in a free and encouraging political environment, *it is more normal to be unfree.* Sometimes believers are specially picked out for savage treatment; often they simply share in the bitter lot of their fellow countrymen, and in particular face savage repression if they dare to be concerned with human rights and human dignity.

Christians are, of course, called to care about all human beings

who are ill treated and repressed, whether they are Christians or
Moslems, agnostics or communists, fascists or anyone else; it is a
sad partiality which limits our concern to our fellow believers.
Indeed there is a sense in which the church of Jesus Christ will
never be a true world church until we learn, in St. Paul's words,
how to weep with those who weep and to rejoice with those who
rejoice, whether they are of our denomination and faith or not. Any
understanding of Christian responsibilities in the systems and
structures of our late twentieth-century world must include some
assessment of the bitter conditions in which many of our fellow
Christians and our fellow human beings have to serve and live.

It is very easy to develop a "selective conscience." Many radical Christians are rightly indignant about the disgusting conditions
for political prisoners in, say, South Africa or South Korea; they
seem, however, strangely unmoved by equally depressing reports
from North Korea or central Africa. Christian businessmen are
likely to accept evidence about labor camps in the Soviet Union or
pressures on dissidents in Mozambique or Czechoslovakia—they
"show once more where socialism leads to"—but they may try not
to face unpleasant truths about political repression in Asian or
Latin American "free enterprise" societies. There is an honorable
tradition in western history of recognizing brutal and inhuman
regimes for what they are, regardless of whether they are left or
right in political color; the post-1945 arguments in France between
Koestler, Malraux, and Sartre, and the more recent controversies
over postwar Vietnam, are significant examples of this. Christian
people, whether they are radicals or comfortable Republicans,
have to face the terrible facts about the frequent corruption of both
free-enterprise and socialist societies by calculatedly brutal intol-
erance and repression. It is particularly depressing to reckon up
how few of the new independent African states have escaped such
political sickness.

It is indeed an extremely unpleasant business to survey once
again the attacks on personal and religious liberty which we have
seen in this century, and no doubt Christian politicians and business leaders face special temptations to ignore the real state of
affairs in the countries with which they are negotiating or trading.

But if our fellow Christians are suffering beastly atrocities while we live in relative peace and freedom, then the least we can do is to grit our teeth and face the facts. This is not easy psychologically, and we are all sometimes weary of television and newspaper reports of torture and inhumanity, but the world church is more than a fellowship of comfortable happy people.

The Sad Record

By 1931 there were already severe problems about human rights in the Soviet Union, in Italy, and in the Japanese Empire, besides endemic problems in Latin America and in some parts of Eastern Europe. In 1933 the ghastly Nazi persecutions started; though we must always remember that it was the Jews, the Communists, and the homosexuals who suffered first and last and most terribly (and they were often undefended by church people), the pressures on committed Christians soon mounted. The writings of Dietrich Bonhoeffer are only one witness to the appalling dilemmas which respectable middle-class Christian families faced soon after Hitler came to power.

In 1939 the war brought new miseries all over Europe and in Southeast Asia, and despite the liberation of western Europe in 1944 and 1945 the Stalinist regimes proved a heartbreaking disappointment to those who had hoped for a human and decent freedom after the Nazi nightmare. In the last forty years, there have been some gains and many losses, as the valuable annual surveys from Freedom House and the constant stream of reports from Amnesty International indicate.[1] The conditions which political prisoners suffer, and the escalation of police, military, and terrorist violence all over the inhabited globe, make up a horrible list.

Special Pressures on the Laity

We should acknowledge straightway that in such bitter conditions it has often been the clergy rather than the laity who have been the prophets and the martyrs—and all honor to them, not one word to belittle their magnificent witness. Nevertheless, we need to examine not so much the position of the clergy but that of the laity, and for two reasons.

First, even the best studies of the modern church under strain, such as the excellent *Discretion and Valour* by my colleague Trevor Beeson,[2] have concentrated almost entirely on official church leaders and structures. The history of the laity is the forgotten history of the church, and this is especially true of the last fifty years. In addition, there is a special sense in which the laity, working in secular state or capitalist structures and enterprises, caught up in compulsory party or business activities and indoctrinations, dependent on the government or the corporation for wages, houses, promotions, and pensions, are even more vulnerable and less able to take an independent line than their clergy.

Indeed, it is a familiar ploy of totalitarian regimes to separate the clergy from the laity, giving ordained ministers an almost privileged status, even guaranteeing their salaries, restoring church buildings, and providing gasoline coupons for travel— provided of course that they keep to their "proper" job of saying services and conducting funerals, and never offer a word of social criticism. For moderately submissive clergy, life under some repressive governments is different, and sometimes slightly easier, than for the laity, who find that they have in fact only the slenderest rights to practice their faith, even in private and family matters.

The Worst, and the Merely Bad

We can classify these pressures. Many Christian people, it must be said, now live under the fear of hideous and brutal torture— sadistic electric shocks to the genitals, day and night interrogations with drugs, blinding lights, and disorientation techniques, and then indefinite incarceration in foul prison camps. These disgusting treatments may be either for themselves or—most damnably—for their husbands or wives or children.

Beyond the pressures brought about by such horrors, and in many countries which we may still consider more civilized, there are a whole range of other less terrible but still most unpleasant sanctions. The threat of being fired, the loss of a pension, the existence of a blacklist of "unreliable" citizens or employees who will never be promoted, the refusal of university places to the children—all these are very common injustices for many fellow members in the world church.

Such pressures are exercised not only by governments. The unacceptable practices of capitalism still too often include such techniques to quiet anyone who speaks out of turn, whether it be in a giant corporation or a small business firm (which may nevertheless be the major employer in a small town without alternative employment). Large corporations are not always as scrupulous in Asia or Latin America as they must by law be in North America or Europe. Again, major dishonesty and corruption are as pervasive as ever in many parts of the world, and sharp pressures to conform are familiar to many Christian politicians and business and union employees.

Though national and local conventions as to what is reasonably permissible vary, of course, from country to country and culture to culture, a quite unacceptable system of political and commercial graft may horribly entrap and intimidate individual laity. We need to recall older and still powerful tyrannies, such as the Mafia and the continued repression of American blacks, at least in some rural areas. It does not require many beatings for a local fear to grow.

What Can We Do?

Any careful reflection on the harsh conditions which so many of our fellow Christians endure today will surely lead us to a terrible sense of the true horrors and sinfulness of today's world. I shall never forget (and never cease to be grateful for) the terrible, sick-to-the-stomach shocks which I had as a teenager when I first read a book on the Nazi concentration camps, and when I met my first refugees from the barbaric horrors in Europe, just a few hundred miles from quiet suburban London. But simple revulsion should soon give way to more thoughtful and positive conclusions.

In the first place, we should surely be more ready and eager than we are to praise God for his faithful witnesses. Their persistence under appalling pressures is so much more important in the life of the world church (and of the human race) than so many of the things with which we keep ourselves busy—quarrels about prayer books, petty denominational jealousies, and the like. When we begin to understand the true position of many of our fellow believers we shall, I suspect, be less and less able to judge them either for sometimes rather puzzling prophesying and demonstrating or for quiet and even apparently submissive stances. This is not only to acknowledge that we can hardly imagine how we might survive, let alone protest, under such appalling conditions, it is also to begin to understand the terrible dilemmas and confusions which face Christians in such societies, and the nightmare of pressures in which they must under God work out what seem to them the most responsible compromises they can make.

We must understand, too, that to protest is also something of a hard compromise, for it may involve our families and friends and colleagues in appalling dangers and ourselves in plotting and lying and political violence. One of the bravest laymen in Nazi Germany, Reinold von Thadden—later founder of the German *Kirchentag* (church congress)—said of the days under Hitler, "It was not possible to do right," and he was relatively fortunate, for his rank and family helped save him from the worst horrors of the Gestapo, though not from a Soviet camp in Siberia.[3]

We must also admit, with shame and humility, that often our fellow Christians—strong and devout church members—are to be found not among the persecuted but among the persecutors. In Northern Ireland, in South Africa, in Brazil and other Latin American countries, the ranks of the oppressors include many church people, both Catholic and Protestants, "in good standing"; this is a scandal which we rarely dare to try to understand, and it will not go away if we simply dismiss such people as "nominal believers." The good Lord must often be ashamed of his "official" followers. In many other comfortable church congregations (in Europe and North America, as well as in South Africa or South America) there is at least latent racism and prejudice which easily supports harsh treatment of unpopular minorities and prisoners ("extremists," "communists"), or persuades us to turn aside from praying for them. We have to remember here the strength of common upper-middle-class prejudices against radicals and radical fellow Christians, which are sometimes quite as strong as other prejudices of radical and left-wing Christians against "capitalist" Christians.

Information and Publicity

We often forget that those of us who live in the relatively free societies of North America and Western Europe can do several practical things to help. In particular, even moderately influential business and professional travelers need to watch their opportunities here. Martin Conway of the British Council of Churches wrote recently, "I long for all of us who travel in other countries . . . to make time for involvement with local Christians, and to be known and used as ambassadors by our own churches."[4] Distinguished visitors are often kept well away from dissidents and opposition politicians and labor camps and urban slums. No doubt many trade negotiations and governmental conferences require some uneasy compromises with unpleasant regimes. (Are they any more guilty than those who live by the balance of world power and the international trade which they arrange?) A word dropped, a question about Mr. X or Mrs. Y, an indication that bad prison conditions are at least known—there is much evidence that all these have been helpful to prisoners of conscience. Many diplomats (some from very small European countries) have been faithful far beyond the call of duty in asking about political prisoners and in helping refugees.

We cannot here explore in detail the clear duty of Christian industrialists and business people to concern themselves with the local conditions in countries where they have subsidiary plants or major trading networks. The matter is of course exceptionally controversial, in particular in questions about South Africa. The fact that some radical church people are stronger on rhetoric than on facts—indeed denounce "transnationals" and "multis" almost as if they were the modern equivalent of medieval demons— sometimes disguises the very considerable achievement which Christian business people have had in making major American banks and corporations examine much more thoroughly than in the past their role in unpleasantly totalitarian countries. The infuriating smugness of some Christian ethicists on such points, and the naive innocence with which they talk about the realities of international trade, can be much too easy an excuse with which to evade the sharp central point: Christians who have influence in international trade and commerce have a duty to know what is happening in those countries; they must not pretend that matters of human rights, of the exploitation of a labor force, of the banning of social protest, are no concern of theirs.

Such Christian leaders, and indeed all of us, are called to keep faith with those under repression, by seeking to be constantly informed about them, by remembering them in our private prayers and reflections, and by seeing that they are not forgotten in public worship. How often, even now, do those who lead prayers in church services mention, in any but the vaguest and almost casual way, "those who suffer"?

We can make the effort to read and think about conditions in countries like Korea (both North and South) or the USSR or Argentina or Czechoslovakia. A good deal of Christian experience suggests that it may be wiser to concentrate on one country, *whether or not it is in the news at the moment,* than to try to understand prayerfully all the miseries of all the world—that sum of suffering really is part of the mystery of God's sorrows, a mystery we can hardly begin to comprehend or to feel. Missionary societies, Amnesty International, and the PEN Club have shown real sense in asking people to focus on certain areas or certain political prisoners at any one time.

Human Freedom Is Important

Finally, one of the ways of keeping faith with fellow human beings under persecution is to watch very carefully our own standards of personal and political freedom. There is a good deal of loose and dangerous talk from some radical Christians about personal freedom being unimportant to hungry or impoverished people. This really is damnable nonsense. It is not uncommon for certain types of economists and government planners to sweep aside questions of human rights in, say, Indonesia or South Korea, by pointing to the undoubted improvement in some workers' wages and food supply. This is unacceptable. A host of glorious witnesses will rightly call us traitors if we so casually abandon our great heritage of personal liberty. We must watch all the time that we do not develop a partial blindness, ignoring the excesses of some whom we might think of as political or ideological allies. The warning of Sir John Colville, formerly personal secretary to Winston Churchill, is relevant here:

> We live among people with a selective conscience, people who no longer judge on generally acknowledged grounds of right and wrong

but consciously or unconsciously make heroes of those whom one political group or another finds ideologically acceptable, and allow no merit at all to the miscreants on the other side of the fence. The rulers of Chile, Spain or South Africa are detestable to some: those of the Soviet Union, Cuba or Czechoslovakia are no less detestable to others.[5]

Indeed, one of the most important things for Christians in the West to do is to encourage and to honor those people and agencies who let us know what is happening, who let us know about the threats to religious and political freedom which are developing in our own countries and elsewhere. I am thinking not only of religious bodies like the National Council of Churches or the Roman Catholic Justice and Peace groups, but also of those politicians who are prepared to take up unpopular causes when it might pay them to pretend that they are too busy, of those lawyers who, often at considerable personal risk, defend political prisoners, and of the national and international corps of journalists, working both in the press and in radio and television.

No doubt the news media sometimes exaggerate reports of brutality, for sadism and violence sell well; no doubt reports from Africa or Eastern Europe are sometimes influenced by propaganda clichés about atrocities (always committed by the other side); but by and large threats to human rights, abuses of personal liberty, and cruel and degrading conditions of employment are still chronicled for us clearly and devastatingly not by church organizations or government information agencies but by the secular journalists of the Western world. We need to honor them for this, we need to heed their warnings, and we must watch all the time for attempts to cripple their freedom to report and to publish.

PART TWO

HOW TO GROW IN RESPONSIBILITY

4

Help from the Local Church

> Consecrated ignorance is not adequate service to God. We may be sensitive to human suffering but at the same time actually increase misery by uninformed ways of dealing with it.
>
> HARVEY SEIFERT, *Power Where the Action Is*

> Disciples can't be copycats.
>
> MICHAEL H. TAYLOR

To be effective in difficulties Christians need more than a simple commitment to Jesus Christ. They need opportunities for growing theologically and spiritually in the same serious way in which they continually develop their secular expertise and skills. We have too many corporation executives with a simple Sunday-school understanding of their faith, too many high ranking military officers with a strong but narrow and undeveloped pietism. All secular corporations and institutions know today that the price of survival and of progress is to *invest* in their people, to spend hard cash and precious time in seminars, conferences, even in retreats, so that in the future there will be informed and alive people to keep their organization going and to reform it intelligently. One clear reason for the weakness of the churches in developing their laity is that they have never learned to invest in them in the same thorough and costly way. The clergy have, at least in North America, a pretty thorough academic and pastoral training, and after ordination they quite rightly expect to enjoy study time, sabbaticals, training conferences, and spiritual retreats at intervals throughout the rest of their lives. A similar investment in the laity would transform the spiritual and theological strength of the churches.

It is also unfortunate—and rather extraordinary—that the very people who are in the front line of secular decision making and (maybe) compromising and politicking are those for whom the churches provide the *least* opportunity for adult Christian education, for intelligent spiritual formation, and for self-development as mature and reasonably confident believers. Those who to God's glory sing in church choirs or help with children's religious education often find rather good opportunities for learning and for training. Those who aspire to help with worship services, with stewardship campaigns, with youth programs, these too may be invited to diocesan or denominational training programs to suit their needs. But those who serve their Lord primarily in their business or political or scientific work, where there are many teasing problems of Christian discipleship not to be wafted away by a simple text or a moral homily, those are precisely the church members who seem to be most neglected by the educational structures of the churches.

Such neglect is, however, rather too easily used as an excuse by laity who find themselves ill equipped to face the strains and ambiguities of modern life. Maybe the local church does not offer much help, maybe the denomination seems more worried about clergy pensions than about the problems of the national economy, maybe even if it does take an interest in economic and social questions the statements seem rather amateurish and unhelpful. Nevertheless, an adult Christian is responsible under God for his or her own self-education and growth in the Spirit, and it is just a cop-out to blame somebody else—whether it is the local clergy or the denominational executives. I suspect that almost all Christian families have something to learn from the intense sense of obligation in Jewish families which has driven them, sometimes under most terrible difficulties, to transmit the depths of their faith to the next generation. I maintain that there is an equal obligation on Christians to work out for themselves (and maybe their children) both a proper respect for the Christian tradition and a proper understanding as to how to modify it to fit what the Spirit is saying to us today. We must accept responsibility for our own Christian development, and we must find help in our own self-education where we can.

Obviously and rightly we ought to be able to find at least some help in our local churches. Americans are really very fortunate here, compared with the shrinking of many a European congregation into a tiny, sometimes rather unattractively narrow-minded group around a faithful but not always outward-looking priest or pastor. Despite the rather ominous reports of the increasing numbers of American Christians who do not now have any very lively connection with any church at all (especially in the major cities),[1] there are still tens of thousands of strong, well-financed, well-staffed congregations in the United States, and in them it ought to be possible to offer a good deal of affirmation, support, and education for laity out in the world. The wealthy congregations of southeastern Connecticut, of Grosse Pointe, Michigan, of Dallas, Texas, of suburban Washington are capable, if they so wish, of doing a very great deal to develop spiritually those business executives and those government officials who still rather faithfully turn up and pay up, Sunday by Sunday, despite the heavy demands on their time. Indeed some busy laity, feeling themselves committed to Sunday church for the sake of their families and children, are much more interested in making the most of Sunday morning than they are in attending midweek events. The period from 9:30 A.M. to 12 noon can include a good deal more than a traditional worship period and coffee hour, as several excellent parish experiments such as Sunday Morning Academies have shown.[2]

What then can a local church do to help their secularly involved laity? Perhaps it ought to be emphasized again that this is not at all the same question as that important one, ''What can the laity do to help in the witness and life of the local parish?'' Of course lay people have a clear responsibility to be active in local church life so far as they can, but in this book we are dealing particularly with those lay people who by reason of their overwhelming public and business responsibilities may not easily find time to serve on local church councils, to help with parish fund raising, or to consider whether or not there should be changes in the forms of Sunday worship. Though it is a very hard thing for overworked clergy to admit (there needs to be serious study of the built-in emphasis on parish life which dominates clergy from the moment they enter seminary), it is sometimes true that in working out the responsible compromises which fill their crowded diaries and weekly schedules, *the laity must give priority to secular responsibilities.* We have too many laity who neglect business, political, labor union, or local community meetings because of church demands on their spare evenings. If "mission" is to take precedence over "maintenance," then local churches—and national synods too—may sometimes have to say, "We cannot expect X to serve on that committee: he is busy three nights a week on political affairs, and he must have some time for family and leisure. We must find a retired woman to take the place of Y: she is really important on the district school board and we must willingly release her from the stewardship committee."

A Variety of Options

Our question for this chapter, "What can the local church give to (rather than demand from) its strongest secular laity?" demands a wide range of answers because of the very wide variations in parish styles in North America. A fine Texas parish, with a million dollars worth of buildings, a well-trained staff, and a reasonably active membership of seven hundred people, or a prosperous Minnesota congregation with plenty of young people and families, is very different from a struggling congregation of elderly people (which nevertheless expects the attendance of its successful sons and daughters), or a moderately viable but tiny Colorado or Ontario country parish. Nevertheless, it is worth saying clearly and emphatically (especially as in the next chapter there is emphasis on nonparish Christian organizations) that, though all residential parishes have now lost their monopoly of Christian organization and education, a reasonably active local congregation still remains an extremely important structure for many laity. Many of the experimenters in new forms of Christian community and outreach ought to have acknowledged this a little more readily.

Parish clergy and church councils who openly and constantly recognize and honor the vocation of the laity in the world can have an extraordinarily valuable influence as they plan the worship, preaching, and teaching of the congregation; and those who significantly deny that vocation, or neglect to affirm it constantly, can have a deeply depressing and frustrating effect. I am convinced that for many laity, but not all, the main strengths of a local church should be in worship and in education—with an obligation for some kind of evangelism, some attempt (not necessarily in traditional forms) to share the good news of the faith with others. If the flavor of the worship and the church education of both children and adults does not positively *affirm* Christian life in the structures of secular society, then there will be definite and disastrous negative effects.

Let us consider ritual and worship first, for they are very powerful in the formation and development of all laity, as of all clergy. Habits, customs, and rituals in worship—whether Baptist or Roman Catholic—teach a great deal, either right or wrong. If the praise and prayer and intercessions of a Sunday service only speak of local and churchly concerns (praying for a bishop, but not for a government official), if other denominations in the town are never mentioned in prayer or in the notices, if the Holy Communion is celebrated without any recognition of Christians under strain or persecution, then everybody from senior citizens to little children will get the feeling, Sunday by Sunday, and year by year, that the church is essentially a little local holy huddle. If, on the other hand, the world outside, the world church, the national and international and ecumenical scene outside the local church walls—if all these things are continually referred to and prayed and rejoiced about, then the members will come to see and to honor the connections and the tensions between Christian discipleship and everyday life. If priests or pastors still do "the whole thing" and perform the whole service (as so often in both Catholic and Protestant congregations), if they always lead the praying and praising, read the Scriptures, conduct the whole of the Communion service, then the work of worship becomes too easily just a matter of their specialist skills. However, if, as in more and more congregations nowadays, laity are active in prayer and worship, in offering prayers and readings, and (as most gloriously on Iona and in many Protestant churches) in helping their neighbors to partake at Holy Communion, then worship becomes an activity of the whole people of God. But it must still be designed not to reflect just the concerns of an ingroup of churchly laity who meet the minister very regularly.

More Substantial Preaching

Preaching and proclamation of God's truth is still, in all its different styles, an important activity for local congregations. I should like to make a plea here for a middle way between the overwhelming reverence still given to a pastor's preaching in some Christian traditions and the sloppy chattiness to which many other services are now reduced. I am dubiously convinced when clergy (often young ones) tell me that they have to spend two or three mornings a week preparing their short Sunday sermons, for the results often seem not to justify such prodigious preparation; but I am a great deal more restless about the silly little talks which are all that some persons offer us nowadays and which are an insult to any adult laity, let alone those with great secular ability. As Max Warren wrote very finely in his lectures to preachers:

> Men expect of us, and rightly expect of us, that we shall know our subject and be able to explain it. They may reject our explanation. What is much more serious is if they reject us because they are more than a little suspicious that we haven't worked at our subject. They will quickly recognise the authority of a man who knows what he is talking about."[3]

I am not asking for a learned lecture, which would be quite out of place in any local church worship, but for something more than seven minutes of banalities. It simply is not true that lay people—whatever their jobs and education—will take only such snippets; some evangelical congregations in both Britain and North America put the rest of us to shame with their careful teaching-and-learning sermons. As Urban T. Holmes has written out of rather another tradition, "If a congregation did only one other thing aside from the representation of those events which called it into being, it should be the training of its membership to think theologically."[4]

Again, it is strange how few clergy ever consult a group of laity about a plan of sermons, or a given topic, before they prepare for, say, Lent or Advent. Yet, if preaching is an activity of the entire congregation, and not just a performance by the cleric, why should this not be a normal practice? Why so little evaluation of preaching after it has taken place? No doubt a parson will, in case of disagreement, have some right to the last word—sermons are not finally drafted by committees—but even then it would be gracious to recognize that he or she is aware of some contrary comments. The essential thing is that the whole work of proclaiming, preaching, and teaching should not be the monopoly, nor the heavy responsibility, of the clergy alone; in some suitable way congregations must join with them in this task. This should, from time to time, include busy and secular laity, for this may be part of their obligation to worship.

Sunday preaching is one of the few monological kinds of teaching left; again and again this has been recognized, and again and again it continues. (What do the specialists in preaching at the theological colleges and seminaries teach their students about this?) There are all kinds of ways of organizing comments and "feedback" on a sermon. Some churches do manage the considerable achievement of having a question-and-answer session in the midst of worship; other congregations achieve no more than a rather embarrassing period when few contributions are offered by anyone. It may or may not be suitable to have comments offered during the service. It may be much more helpful (as a good many congregations have found) to organize a coffee-and-questions group after worship, especially if church school for the children has not yet finished. Sometimes a group can drive off to a nearby home for prelunch drinks. Not everybody wants to join in this kind of thing, but Christian proclamation is more than a matter of enunciating unquestionable dogmas; the art of Christian learning like the art of worship, is surely something a parish must take great trouble over.

The topics of sermons are important. It is not that the laity want to study the problems of Indonesia or of unemployment every Sunday, indeed they often hunger most for more substantial teaching about the Bible and about Christian doctrine. Preaching about Indonesia or the Bible or anything else must reflect the fundamental doctrine of the laity as responsible witnesses in the secular world. This is not just a matter of problems and denunciations, there must be also an affirmation of the glorious vocation of Christian people. All too often in listening to preaching I have detected the following assumptions, which make intelligent and responsible laity grit their teeth or go to sleep: (1) The highest vocation for a Christian is to be an ordained minister. (2) The really dedicated way for lay Christians to serve God is to engage in congregational or other church work. (3) If there is to be any social action, the best way to do it is to form or support a parish group, or a denominational group, or (reluctantly) an ecumenical group. There is little mention of other civic or professional voluntary groups, and even less about witnessing in the present structures of secular society, where the laity are week by week.

The same dangerous presuppositions can be found, again and again, in church school and youth programs. Yet from the earliest days when children are assimilating television and other news of the outside world, right through to programs for adults and senior members of the congregations, only that teaching and learning which recognizes and honors the work of Christian laity in the secular world can rightly take the name of Christian education. Again, Lay Schools of Theology and parish Lent series do not necessarily have always to be on social problems or international crises, they do have to reflect a positive affirmation of lay ministries in the world.

If a parish is reasonably prosperous and strong, then it can do much more, especially if it can be generous and cooperate with other local congregations instead of remaining aloof from them. Far too many Lent or Advent courses are rather inadequate and thin (and certainly do not attract the strong laity with whom this book is concerned), while often in the same suburb or even the same street, other congregations are running similar series of meetings. It has always amazed me how ineffective some local councils of churches and ministerial associations are in cooperating to produce first-class adult education programs—one of those things which surely all Christians (from Roman Catholics to Salvation Army members) are allowed to undertake together. In many such programs to be ecumenical would be economical in the use of buildings and heating and speakers and films and other resources. It is the sheer inefficiency of so many little programs in so many unattractive church buildings which makes busy laity more than a little exasperated with local parish life.

The Clergy as
Educational Advisers

A local congregation simply cannot cover the wide spectrum of human occupations and interests from computer specialists to teachers of children, but surely local pastors have to keep a careful record of the laity's interests and responsibilities in work, politics, and leisure. If they don't, how can they ever understand the outreach of the parish, or plan the worship and prayers of the congregation? Let them also keep a record of all the opportunities available for Christian growth and education in that particular region—whether organized by their particular denomination or by any other. (Let us hope that they at least know what their clerical brethren and sisters are up to.) Let them try to match different lay people's interests with the opportunities available, whether inside or outside their particular parish or neighborhood. No doubt if church members have special problems about marriage styles or bereavement, then their local parish may be able to help, particularly if it joins with a neighboring church and pools the resources of clergy and laity. If a parish has a banker or a medical specialist or a journalist in the congregation, it cannot hope to offer them much specialist Christian education for their specialist responsibilities. It ought then to be able to say, "Here is a good congress/course/ group on your topic, organized by the local Industrial Mission/the diocese/the Roman Catholic retreat house/the Presbyterian Synod. Why not go along and try it? Indeed why not 'represent' the parish, and give us a report when it is over?"

Which is to say that many local clergy ought to be educational advisers to the laity, rather than educational monopolists, just as in the secular world teachers must gladly let students move on to all kinds of specialist courses which they cannot themselves offer. The role of ordained ministers and priests as thoughtful enablers of the laity has been developed very sensitively by some recent writers, notably by James Fenhagen in his book *Mutual Ministry*.[5] What is distressing is that many clergy still do not see themselves in such a role, and that those who do lack the practical skills and information which can make them really helpful. In particular, they often know little of opportunities offered to the laity by other denominations—even in their town or neighborhood—or by specialist or residential centers.

One of the best thing which a local church can do for some laity, especially the younger, not yet wealthy but promising people (who are often sent on business or scientific courses), is to offer them modest scholarship or travel costs to Christian conferences and seminars to enable them to match their growth in secular skills and knowledge with some theological and biblical wisdom. Why should it be so often only the ordinands and clergy who are given travel grants for their further education?

Finally, and most importantly, a local congregation will be of great benefit to able, influential, responsible laity precisely because it is *not* entirely composed of such people! Hans-Ruedi Weber of the World Council of Churches has several times pointed out that such Christians, often upper middle-class in style and education, need the constant reminder that they are not the only "important" believers, and though some suburban white parishes tend to be elitist in this bad sense, there is in many parishes, Catholic or Protestant, a wide range of ability and interests which can be an educational experience in itself. As Gabriel Moran has put it, "We urgently need education by adults for adults to become more adult," but central to his whole thesis of true Christian adulthood is that it is more than secular skills or intellectual ability.[6] Even more than this, a sincere membership in a local worshiping community, a regular experience of Holy Communion together with fellow believers of all kinds and abilities is to find, as Hans

Küng has movingly written, "a spiritual home in which we can find the great questions of the whence and the whither, the why and wherefore, of man and the world."[7]

Informal Local Groups

All this is to suggest that the traditional parish still has a major role to play in encouraging and supporting and challenging the kind of laity with which this book is concerned. But it has lost its old village monopoly as a transmitter and developer of the Christian tradition, and it must learn to live positively with all kinds of other Christian activities. Otherwise it will simply become (as so often in Europe it already has) a satisfying concern for a strictly limited number of laity who like that kind of local, rather cozy, religious style, while very many other nonparish Christians will be increasingly separated from organized church life and worship of any kind.

Indeed it is important that we consider briefly another common phenomenon these days: the growth of all kinds of house groups, intentional communes and communities, and other meetings for informal Christian worship. These are often cranky, esoteric, temporary, cliquey, heretical, irregular, and infuriating to established church denominations and parishes, but they do help many of the more secular and unconventional laity! Though many such experiments do not last long, others take their place, and this movement is now, all over the Western world, a clear option for many younger professional and business people who wish to affirm or to discover the Christian faith but find traditional parish life unsatisfying. There needs to be much more thorough investigation, both in the United States and in Europe, into how these informal groups may, on the one hand, be free to experiment in many different ways, and on the other, not lose altogether their connection, and indeed their Christian fellowship, with other members of the body of Christ grouped in more traditional structures and denominations. I do not say this at all so that they may be "claimed and caught" by the great traditional churches, but because on their own they are often temporary and weak and faddish. They need contact with other Christians, with the great traditions of Christian wisdom and learning, they need resources for the teaching of their children, the opportunity to help in the development of Christian wisdom for the future. Something is often achieved by informal discussions and by the publication of articles and books, but there can be a rather "holier than thou" flavor about such groups which suggests that they, too, need to admit that theirs is not the only possible style of Christian living. It is also fair to say that some of the delightfully informal groups and house churches are a little parasitic upon the formal churches. They often have a leader or minister or priest who has had expensive (if unsatisfying) theological training. The members have had much Christian education and experience as children or adults in the churches they have left or are leaving. What is to happen for the future?

Perhaps there should be an affiliation between such groups and a local council of churches (with any membership fees properly paid). Sometimes experimental groups link more naturally with a denominational body—a parish, a district organization, or a national organization (like the orders within Roman Catholic and Anglican traditions). There should be positive experiments and discussions about possible affiliation, the fees to be paid, and the services to be obtained. Maybe from time to time there should be a major rally or service in a great church or cathedral for both the formal and the informal parishes, without any private reservations about either being the only style of Christian community and organization acceptable to Almighty God. But so far—especially in the older denominations where traditional stiffness may make such breakaway groups more likely—there has been more backbiting than constructive discussions on these points.

The Parish Must Limit Its Demands

There are indeed other important things which a parish or informal group may do for its busy laity. It must sometimes get out of their way! A parish in East Manchester, England, had a surprising rule for its adult members: There were to be no evening meetings or functions during the week. On Sunday morning, there were all sorts of things—a Eucharist, a tea and coffee break, discussions, parish meetings—but not during the week. The members of this small but strong inner-city parish were to be "liberated," set free to go into all kinds of secular groups and activities—union meetings, school committees, political rallies, and the like.[8] So many prosperous suburban parishes, both in Britain and in North America, still try to entangle their laity in church clubs, groups, or choir practices, night after night, so that they have no chance to be human with other human beings who are not church members. Those who attend a medical or a business meeting are made to feel a little disloyal, as if they were graded as less keen church members, whereas they are the very Christians who may be called to serve as the salt in the secular world. This is not to say that such laity have no obligation to the parish to which they belong; it is to say that they must often be free to do other things in what leisure time they have. If they are not officially released, and indeed encouraged, to such work outside the parish, then they will probably undertake it anyway and drift away altogether from church membership, like so many hundreds of thousands of other Christians.

One of the most ridiculous examples of such tensions between parish and other Christian obligations was shown by a group of business people I once met at 7:30 on a Monday morning. They were serious, committed senior laity (entirely awake and alert at such a time). They tried very hard to meet the obligation to join in this group each week before they jetted all over the map on their executive concerns. But the minister made a rather pathetic plea that they join in parish clubs on Tuesdays and Thursdays and a parish supper on Friday night. They looked uneasy, perhaps a trifle guilty, and there was not a hope in hell that they could fulfill his expectations of parish loyalty. He should have known better.

Help Outside the Local Church

The people are growing: the structure lags behind.

SARA CHARLES

People with a spark of genius often have ignition trouble.

Graffiti, Vancouver *Province*

No matter how much the local church may help in the support and development of the laity of the future, it is undeniable that it lost long ago any claim to be the only place for Christian education and nurture. The clergy, in particular, have long insisted in specialist theological colleges and continuing education courses for themselves. It is strange that for so long it has been assumed that adult education for the laity can be carried on almost exclusively in the local congregation, rather as if secular education for the bulk of the people had never developed beyond the village school or the "little red schoolhouse" of American history.

It is notable that Roman Catholic and, to some extent, Anglican/Episcopal traditions have been more helpful to laity development. It has always been assumed by these churches that there will be retreat houses which laity may attend, that there may be "third orders" or lay associates of many of the great international religious movements like the Franciscans or the Benedictines, that there may be nonparochial laity with special professional concerns like physicians and lawyers. Other denominations have often organized summer conferences and holiday centers, but have been less ready to acknowledge that the laity may wish to have continuous nonparish, and even nondenominational, activities. Yet the experiences of the last quarter century, both in Europe and in North America, have indicated the enormous value and legitimacy of many kinds of Christian learning and fellowship other than those in parish organizations. The church of Jesus Christ is richly multiple in form today, not only in denominations but also in the wide variety of its experiments in learning and witnessing outside the residential parishes.

This is especially true for those Christians who are called, in the terms of this book, to positions of major and complicated responsibilities. Many of the worries and dilemmas of business or government leaders are complex and detailed; though the Sunday sermon or the Lenten discussion group in a local church may effectively highlight some of the general biblical and ethical principles involved, it is extremely unlikely to be able to dig deeply into the particular complications of being, for example, an executive in a multinational oil firm or a union leader in a jurisdictional dispute. Yet, as William Blake insisted, "He who would love his neighbour must do so in minute particulars," and deep digging must be undertaken, if Christians are to advance beyond pious theological generalities. It is often in nonparochial, nonlocal groups that they can overcome the serious intellectual weaknesses which have so often hampered Christian social thinking in recent years.

Such groups are often criticized (especially by those who in fact lack the ability to join them) as elitist in the wrong sense. It is quite possible that they may become spiritually or intellectually proud, that they may blame the decline of the dollar or the increase in urban crime on lazy workers or pleasure-loving citizens. But it is also possible for these groups and for church leaders generally to be so inhibited by sloppy guilt feelings about being overprivileged and overeducated that they fail to render the one special service which they may be able to offer to the church and to the world, that of *thinking* clearly and sharply as well as *feeling* intensely about theological and social questions. Of course they must make every effort to empower and encourage representatives of minority groups, of ordinary workers, of nonintellectual people to make their case and to join in the search for the mind of Christ, but there are many problems in church and society where simple and earnest goodwill is not enough.

Not Much Progress in Thirty Years

Such arguments for specialized laity groups were common enough in the years immediately after World War II; and indeed the 1950s saw, both in Europe and in the United States and Canada, a great many experimental centers for laity education, of which the lay academies in the Federal Republic of Germany are particularly famous. More details about these developments may be found in *God's Lively People*[1] and in the crop of books which appeared in those years. However, it must be admitted at once that in North America, with certain admirable exceptions, these programs did not really succeed in helping very much Christians in positions of major responsibility. Without in any way wishing to discount what were, in many instances, most valuable experiments (neglected and given far too little encouragement from the major churches), the best way we can benefit from their experiences is to see what we can now learn from their struggles and difficulties.

One sharp lesson for us is that they often suffered, and in many cases closed down, because of "benign neglect" from church denominations and budget committees. The history of industrial ministries in the United States over the last twenty years is largely a story of smaller and smaller grants from church sources, so that their fine work has been financed far below the level of true effectiveness. Two examples of that are the Boston Industrial Mission's work at the cutting edge of all kinds of technological and industrial problems in the laboratories and corporations around Route 128, and Cameron P. Hall's work with the laity groups associated with the National Council of Churches.

In Britain, a survey of church staffs in Teesside (in Northeast England) showed recently that some 300 clergy in that area were devoted to parish ministries, and that only *eight* were released for developing a prophetic ministry to the great industries of the region. It is distressing to find that the Ecumenical Center in Brussels is so minimally financed that it cannot adequately develop a sensitive and informed Christian presence as the European Community

moves ahead with its massive and growing responsibilities. These
are European examples, but many nonparish groups in North
America—the urban work in Toronto, the attempts at a Wall Street
ministry in New York, some of the specialist groups in Berkeley,
California—have been equally starved of funds.

Many denominations faced with financial problems (when will
they not have them?) first of all cut their grants to experimental,
nonparochial, maybe ecumenical programs: they are not regarded
as part of the "essential" activities of the churches. It may well be
that in the long run, many programs for responsible laity can be
largely financed by the laity themselves (who do, after all, normally
enjoy rather good incomes and are often taught to "value what you
pay for"), but to start to develop such programs with style and skill
and accurate background information demands not lavish but certainly adequate financing. Often the clergy enablers or secretaries
of such groups are all too evidently overworked and underin-
formed, strong on passionate social conviction and weak on their
background reading. Surely the generous giving and pledging of
upper-middle-class laity to their churches and denominations gives
them the right to claim adequate support for nonparish programs
which can help them.

I suspect that another weakness of many city or regional programs for the laity has been a certain lack of confidentiality. I can
think of one city group for business leaders and of another for
scientists that became rather too much publicized, as if the "important" Christians concerned could be claimed as denominational scalps. (There, surely, is a wrong kind of elitism.) Just as
with secular "think tanks," there may be an obligation to let some
conclusions and comments be released eventually for general discussion and criticisms, but there is much value in allowing relaxed,
informal, off-the-record comments—from Christians, muddled
Christians, and non-Christians—without clumsy and premature
publicity. Some of the work at the best laity centers (like Bad Boll
and Tutzing in the Federal Republic of Germany, and those in
Washington, D.C., Toronto, Scotland, and Northern Ireland) has
only succeeded, as I see it, because of a firm respect for confidentiality and a readiness of church people not to claim any

special credit for the programs concerned. We must always remember that Christian learning necessarily involves the participants in serious and sometimes painful readjustments of belief and values and life-styles; these are not easily achieved in the glare of publicity.

It is also clear now that the great wave of sensitivity training and of encounter sessions in Christian adult education has not had unambiguous results in the last fifteen years. Of course it has often been valuable for rather stuffy and rigid Christian thinkers—theologians, business people, scientists—to learn the value of informal and nonverbal "encounters," but sometimes this gain has been distorted into a facile antiintellectual mood—"we feel good about the blacks"—rather than *analyzing* the bitter inequalities of the urban ghettos. Sometimes there has been a real arrogance in the trainers concerned (often, it must be said, clergy), who have not always remembered that the secular world has been making its own experiments and assessments of these various kinds of learning processes. Sometimes encounter groups have been so intent on their own learning and loving together, or on their personal relationships at home or with other individuals, that they have almost ignored the structural and organizational problems of our modern world, with which politicians, business people, and social leaders must be concerned. It may be suggested, for instance, that the fine chain of United Church laity centers across Canada has been much more successful with family and personal problem conferences than with events offering support to those laity who have to run business or governmental organizations. Those centers may certainly reply that they cannot do everything in laity education, and that they do best to concentrate on the kind of work they have proved they can do well. Fair enough, but in that case the United Church of Canada, like many American churches, does need to develop a parallel series of programs which minister especially to those engaged in "structural ministries," working inside the organizations and bureaucracies of that great country. It is much to be hoped that the pioneering series of laity seminars organized by the same United Church can be expanded and developed.[2]

The Way Forward

These are some of the lessons which we may learn from the achievements, partial achievements, and partial failures of the last twenty-five years. I believe that we can now see more clearly a good pattern for nonparish support for the kind of laity with which this book is primarily concerned.

In the first place, such nonparish work needs to be accepted and indeed affirmed by the various churches and their leaders. In the early days of the academies in Germany and of various laity centers in Britain and North America, there were unfortunate tensions between the parishes and denominational machinery and the eager (sometimes rather arrogant) leadership of the new experiments. Surely now we can hope for a better kind of partnership between parish and nonparish ministries. And here, surely (as we saw in the last chapter) the attitude and training of parish clergy is all-important. If local ministers and bishops and superintendents can catch a vision of the work and ministry of the whole church (and not just of their part of it), and if they can not merely tolerate but actually encourage laity to experience both parish and nonparish styles of Christian learning and fellowship, then the whole body will grow. I can remember with some gratitude various parish priests in England, in the 1940s and 1950s, who tolerated my joining various informal and ecumenical Christian groups, and, in particular, my increasing involvement in the Iona Community in Scotland. But they could have been a bit more enthusiastic, instead of hinting that I should be a little more loyally Anglican and that I ought more seriously to consider ordination so that I could really do Christian work. I am sure that a parish priest or minister ought to rejoice when the laity undertake ecumenical or nonparish learning together.

What kinds of nonparish activities will be particularly helpful to responsible laity under strain? I suggest three: (1) opportunities for retreats which are appropriate for their needs; (2) opportunities for dialogue and argument about their special responsibilities; (3) opportunities for some kind of Christian brainstorming about the future.

There is no doubt that lay people today are expressing a need for opportunities for spiritual retreats and times for reflection, more than in past decades. This is not just a matter of the pressures of secular life and decision making; they have always been severe and it is not really clear that they are worse now than in the 1930s. It is more a stirring of the Spirit, a God-given hunger for a deeper spirituality, which is evident (according to various opinion polls in Britain and in the United States) both among churchgoers and among that very considerable fringe group of Christians who are not convinced church members.

The difficulty is that retreats—whether Roman Catholic or Protestant—tend to fall into one of two categories, neither of which are especially helpful to busy decision makers. Some are still traditional in style, which will suit Christians accustomed to and comfortable with that style. That's fine, but it is likely that now, as in past generations, only a small minority of active Christians will appreciate them and gain in spiritual strength from them. Others are popular, contemporary, perhaps sentimental, perhaps guitarish, perhaps a little trivial spiritually. They are sometimes open to the accusation that they do not take spiritual troubles seriously enough! It is also a problem common to both kinds of retreats that they deal primarily with matters of faith and with personal and family relationships, which is entirely legitimate providing that they make this clear and do not claim that this is the whole of the challenge of the gospel. Certainly business people and politicians have as many such questions to face as anyone else.

Nevertheless, there is a great need in many areas for the kind of retreat center which will both cater to the personal problems of responsible people and minister to their particular spiritual strains as they try to make their faith real in their occupations and their public involvements. Wise parish clergy will know about such centers (whatever denomination runs them) and will quietly suggest that executive people, above all, need from time to time such a withdrawal from their usual hectic life-styles. Maybe a good rule of thumb is: once a year with your spouse and family, once a year on your own. Albert van den Heuvel, the former Secretary of the Dutch Reformed Church in the Netherlands, has even suggested that in the future such a practice may be more important than Sunday churchgoing. We do not need to concede this point to see the very real value of a weekend apart, at say one of those admirable Roman Catholic centers which have moved into new styles of retreats, or at a place like Holden Village in eastern Washington, or Iona, where one is able to work out one's own timetable of worship, silence, reflection, and dialogue.

There is now a great deal of evidence for the value of various kinds of professional and occupational groups to business executives, medical doctors, architects, and so on. The thirty years experience of the European lay academies and of the Faith and Life Institutes of the Lutheran Church in America, organized by Harold C. Letts,[3] are clear evidence that, though these are not themselves total Christian education (their sponsors have never really suggested this), they are invaluable in developing and refining the Christian discipleship of business and professional people. Sometimes, as in much of the German and Dutch and Swiss work, these groups will meet in special residential facilities, sometimes, as with the Lutheran Institutes or the activities of the Christian Frontier Council in London, England, they will use rented accommodations or just meet for a series of evening sessions.

From the varied experiences of many such groups all over the world, we can now gain some clear hints for future developments.

1. It may often be necessary to limit the group to people with genuine ability. So much Christian adult education work is "middle, middle, middle"—just for people who are middle-aged, middle class, and of middle ability. Such a limitation obviously has dangers of the wrong kind of elitism, but these must be faced and risked. Sophistication need not mean a lack of concern for poor or minority people; it may indeed be necessary if, in a complicated world, they are to have justice at all.

This is not at all a justification for some of those all-white, rather paternalistic groups which sometimes bemoan the state of the cities or the poverty of "those people." Minority groups in the United States—blacks, Mexican-Americans, Puerto Ricans— have every right not only to offer topics for the agenda of such groups, but to participate in them. In their communities there are plenty of able people, more skilled in dialogue and in effective arguing than white corporation executives may believe. But to gain their effective cooperation in a specialist Christian group will require much more time and trouble in recruitment than many churches even now are prepared to take. It is indeed very disturbing to find how few church leaders seem competent to consider the responsibilities of, for instance, black laity with outstanding ability—often now, for reasons good and less good, offered very rapid promotion in corporations and governmental organizations.

2. It is absolutely essential that the staff members (clergy or laity) for such groups be very competent. They must have genuine skill in personal and group relationships, and a real ability to *listen* to the arguments developed and to respond to them. So often theological consultants for such groups lack this skill. I remember one dialogue among criminologists in Washington, D.C., which was almost ruined by the determination of the theologian in the group to plow through a faded seminary lecture. On the other hand, I can recall with admiration several groups of politicians and lawyers, both in Europe and in California, where with great courtesy and flair the theologian present reacted to the problems expressed in the discussions and genuinely helped everyone to see where the gospel might relate to them. Such resource people must also have considerable background knowledge of the secular disciplines under consideration. Boldern Academy near Zurich, Switzerland, is outstanding for the way in which it allows its staff people time to keep up in a secular field, such as politics, union affairs, or medical developments.

In the great days of William Temple College at Rugby, England, it was the same. As Miss E. M. Batten, then Principal, wrote:

You must know your stuff, Christianwise, and yet be on the frontier of secular knowledge too. So everybody on your staff has got to work very hard, and do a lot of reading. Keep up theologically, keep on the frontiers, keep alive, and keep open enough to be challenged by the people who are coming to the center you operate. We built up our staff on the basis that each member would have some academic discipline of their own, some theological competence, and also have held down a job in one of our special areas of interest.[4]

3. The question of recruitment is of the greatest importance. Sometimes an experiment which is swamped by "average" church laity will never attract or satisfy really able people, who are also extremely busy people and rightly infuriated if the church wastes their time. Again, the German academies have much to teach us here. They have developed various methods of recruiting people through the secular structures of a city and the networks of an industry or a profession, rather than just through parish clergy, which may produce first-class choir members rather than people of competence on the question under discussion.

4. It is important for such a group to be able not only to set its own agenda and to enjoy a congenial environment (sometimes a motel is more appropriate than a very "churchly" center), but also to start from its own jargon and literature and style of work. For instance, if one examines the secular literature on nuclear studies, urban planning, or futurology, one soon finds there serious questions about ethics and human values. It is important to build on such secular references, even if they are better known by the lay people than by the theologians present.

5. Almost all these groups should be exercises in practical ecumenism, including members not only from mainstream Protestant churches, but also Roman Catholics, Jews, and nonchurch people. It should be emphasized that the term *frontier,* as originally conceived by Dr. J. H. Oldham (who founded the Christian Frontier Council in London, England), does not refer to some kind of barrier or no-man's-land *between* church people and secular experts. It has reference to the new frontiers of human knowledge and experience which God calls church people and others to explore *together.*

6. Some groups have become unnecessarily hung up about demands for "action," and about accusations that they are just engaged in pleasant liberal discussions about public issues. It is certainly true, as in Edward van Hengel's words, that "in our time it may be that uncommitted dialogue is not only foolish but a sin" and that all Christian learning should include a quite stern element of challenge and of commitment to change. It may still be right, however, for many laity to continue in their present secular struc-

tures, changing what they can, protesting when protest will be effective, but operating politically within their present organizations and bureaucracies rather than leaving to form a new *Society for This* or a new *Commune for That.* A Christian frontier or professional group which does not have some element of self-assessment and self-criticism will be flabby; a frontier group which does not recognize the bitter necessity sometimes for responsible compromise will be superficial.

7. Such a group will offer not only opportunities for sharp self-education and mutual criticism, but it will also offer some Christian support for its members. As Walter Lippman wrote years ago, "It is not enough to criticize the official's policy. We must put ourselves under his skin, for unless we have tried to face up to the facts before him, we have produced nothing but holier-than-thou moralizing."

It is clear from the experiences of many such occupational groups that they often become much more than pleasant discussion groups. They develop into genuine Christian fellowships. This kind of growth can be facilitated or impeded by the leadership and the clergy present. I have known some who were far too eager to move to some kind of worship or praying, but also others who were strangely insensitive to a strong desire for such a development on the part of the lay people present. Surely it should be perfectly acceptable for informal Christian discussion and study groups to engage from time to time in informal styles of Christian meditation and worship, not as a substitute for, but as a supplement to, their normal church and denominational practices.

Christian Think Tanks

In their secular wisdom almost all major organizations now indulge (albeit with a proper critical skepticism) in long-range planning, and in brainstorming about the future. Such groups as the Hudson Institute, the Club of Rome, and the various bodies meeting at Aspen, Colorado, are now famous or notorious for the different futures they suggest for humankind. Many Christians in responsible positions are asked by their corporation or government or university departments to join in such exercises, many more are expected to keep up with the literature and the reports which stream from such conclaves. It is distressing that though Roman Catholic, Anglican, and other bishops and church leaders allow themselves the luxury of world meetings from time to time, they are rather slow to offer similar opportunities to the laity. (All honor to the work of Dr. Paul Abrecht and the Church and Society sub-unit of the World Council of Churches, which in its world conferences and in its publications has attempted to face some of the implications of modern technology for all humankind.) It would be wise for the American and German churches, in particular, to invest a certain amount of money in quite ruthless brainstorming sessions, where some of their competent laity and theologians might consider together some of the secular prophecies now circulating about the next hundred years. The Dutch are pioneering here, with their Work Group 2000,[5] but I do not think that the Hudson Institute, for instance, has ever enjoyed a major dialogue with American theologians. I am not talking about a surrender to the latest fads or the "doom and gloom" prophecies common to the second-rate television documentaries; I am asking that the church help some of its laity, at least, to look into the future in a Christian way, just as they are asked by their secular employers to do so in a more commercial and secular way.

PART THREE

SPECIAL OCCUPATIONS AND OPPORTUNITIES

6

Christian Politicians

> The only way in which, in the organized life of society, desirable changes can be brought about, and undesirable changes prevented, is by political action. All talk about a better society is idle daydreaming till it is translated into public policy.
>
> J. H. OLDHAM

> A vast field for the apostolate has opened up in the national and international field, where most of all the laity are called to be stewards of Christian wisdom.
>
> The Decree on the Apostolate of the Laity,
> Second Vatican Council

FOR THE LAST two hundred years or more there has been a strong prejudice among "really committed" Christians—especially among Protestants and evangelicals—which holds that it is almost impossible to be a faithful Christian and a successful politician. This attitude was never quite reconciled with the honor and prestige accorded by the churches to famous statesmen and great war leaders—the devout might assume that some very special providence had protected them from corruption and temptation, the cynical thought it more likely that they had not been found out. The general assumption was that politics was not, as Robert Kennedy claimed, "an honorable profession" for the Lord's people.

Then, from the 1930s onward, the older European tradition that

Christian laity (and clergy too) must not be afraid of power and political responsibility gained strength again. Books by leaders like William Temple in Britain and Reinhold Niebuhr in the United States[1] pointed out the dangers of Christian cowardice, of leaving power to other people, of running away from political decisions, of not voting and leaving the elections to the Nazis and the Communists. After 1945, in both North America and Europe, there was a great concern to have a Christian "presence" in political parties, not only in the so-called Christian-Democrat groups in Western Europe but also in other established political structures.

The situation now, in the early 1980s, is both better and worse. I think it is fair to say that many Christians who in the past would not relate their faith to political and economic affairs now try to make some kind of a relationship. After the Holocaust and the other Nazi atrocities, the revelations about Stalinist communism, the ghastly tragedy of the Vietnam War, and the Watergate scandals, many Christian consciences have been aroused. The extraordinary troubles of President Carter over the hostages in Iran and the Soviet occupation of Afghanistan have stimulated a good deal of hard, and indeed painful, reflection over the role of a very sincere Christian in political and international affairs.

There has been a wave of evangelical concern about political involvement as evidenced by the documents from their conferences at Chicago, Lausanne, and so on.[2] Richard Mouw, a leader in this admirable movement, writes:

> It is not enough to insist, as many conservative evangelical Christians have done, that "changed hearts will change society." If the manipulative patterns which are built into the very structures of social relationships are not changed, all of the effects of sin have not been challenged—and it may be that as a result many "hearts" will not be capable of adequate "change."[3]

Many stodgy pietistic congregations would be surprised to hear of the topics discussed heatedly at such places as Fuller Seminary in California, or Calvin College, Grand Rapids. It is notorious that the most sweetly docile Catholic convents are now infiltrated by all kinds of radical social and political concerns.

Doomed to Corruption?

However, such Christian fervor for a stronger social conscience does not always work to support Christian politicians. There are two contemporary Christian attitudes toward politics and political systems which are unhelpful.

The first, which may be said to embody many of the insights of that distinguished and gloomy French polemicist, Jacques Ellul, is that the political and economic systems of today are fatally corrupt and are doomed, that powerful politicians must necessarily do dreadful things, and that it is naive to be surprised about this. For instance, Ellul claims in his *Betrayal of the West* that "Richard Nixon did what every head of state does today, and everyone knew this."[4] Such a blanket condemnation of "every head of state," such an assumption of universal corruption, is hardly encouraging to those Christians contemplating a career in politics. This is only another, sophisticated way of adopting the old "inevitability of degradation" stance.

A second way of looking at politics and politicians today, which is not really much more helpful, is that of saying that there *is* a Christian style of just politics, which people like President Carter and Chancellor Schmidt could adopt if they really wanted to. Sometimes this "more excellent" way is thought of as a kind of pacifist anarchism, sometimes as a purified idealistic socialism, which seems to have very little to do with the very harsh realities and ambiguities of either social-democratic politics in Western Europe or the regimes of the Soviet bloc or of some African states. Irving Louis Horowitz—no apologist for capitalism—has rightly accused the New Left of suffering from "the alienated sense of being extrinsic to power,"[5] and many Christian writers on politics and world affairs are equally unhelpful and utopian. The assumption is that Christians are entitled to take part in politics *only if they don't compromise,* only if they really stand for absolute Christian Love and Peace and align themselves totally with the poor and the outcast. On such perfectionist radicals, Julian Bond, the distinguished black politician in Georgia, has aptly commented:

> When I offer ideas, they reject them. If I say, "Go to work in political campaigns," they say, "That's bourgeois liberalism." If I say, "Go to work in your neighborhood," they say, "That's paternalism." If I say, "Find a building under construction and if there are no blacks on the crew, stop construction on that building," they say, "That's token change."

What such political "prophets" are really asking for, whether clergy or laity, whether from the *National Catholic Reporter* or from *Sojourners,* is exactly what is impossible for Christians in politics. We must face bitter reality here, as many friends and supporters of President Carter have found. The art of politics is not about utopias, Christian or otherwise; it is about an endless succession of compromises and ambiguities. As President John F. Kennedy often said (quoting the Victorian statesman Lord Morley) it is "one long second best, where the choice often lies between two blunders." To get an appropriation or an effective piece of legislation through the Congress of the United States involves any president or political leader in much "wheeling and dealing" with various power groups, lobbies, and factions, and demands not only great persuasive skills but also the kind of ruthless pressure in which Lyndon Johnson excelled, especially if any reform is to be achieved reasonably quickly.[6] Here McGregor Burns's "transactional leadership," which we noted in chapter 2, is definitely a matter of transactions, of bargains.

They Are Called to Muddy Their Hands

Some of our most sincere social activists in both Europe and North America (perhaps especially in Canada) still need to accept the harsh reality of this analysis. It is entirely right to proclaim strong standards of social justice as a preacher or a teacher or even as an agitator, but these are the privileges (and the temptations) of the "outsiders." To be immersed in politics, to exercise or be confronted with *power,* is a different kind of responsibility. As David Owen, the former British Foreign Secretary, said in 1979 on television, it is the calling, the burden of politicians to "muddy their hands on behalf of the rest of the country."

It is precisely for this that we must honor and support our fellow Christians who are involved in politics. They have chosen to try to exercise power—political, police, military, economic power—as responsibly as they can. They and their allies do win some victories: it was a major achievement that the American political system survived the dreadful strains of the Vietnam War and the excesses of the Nixon administration. It is not true, as Ellul would suggest, that they are inevitably dragged into major corruption; when they are, we need to remember that God does promise grace when we fail, and also that he does seem to value courage of this high order. It is clear that they have chosen a precarious and peculiarly strenuous kind of existence. We must at least try to understand their special difficulties.

In the first place, many of the choices with which they—and their fellow politicians—are faced are all but overwhelming. We do not have to accept the thesis that modern economic and technological systems are "demonic" to realize that their complexity and their interdependence make them extremely difficult to control. (We must not say "impossible.") Even in quiet countries like Denmark or the Netherlands, it is never possible to do all the good that sincere people demand and sincere Christian politicians hope for; people just will not pay the taxes necessary (and this includes many sincere Christians too). In an area like East Glasgow or the South Bronx, in complicated, elderly, battered social structures like northern Britain or Pennsylvania, the list of necessary, urgent, "imperative" reforms is so long that even in days of national prosperity it seems totally impossible to put everything right—and the 1980s do not seem likely to be prosperous and affluent years for the Western nations. It will be easy for church and other reformers to lose patience with the usual democratic political procedures, and to rage against the "system" and the fellow Christians involved in the "system."

We must remember again, as we saw in chapter 3, the far more appalling dilemmas which face Christians politically involved in more authoritarian regimes, or in time of war. The agonized phrase of Albert Camus, "I should like to be able to love my country and to love justice," haunts many of the sleepless nights of Christian

politicians in our time, whether they face the brutalities of Latin
America, the secret police of Eastern Europe or the savage laws of
many African countries. When, if ever, do you agree to lock up
popular agitators and opposition politicians? When, if ever, do you
drop bombs? Even nonnuclear ones? How much money should
you grant for this and that admirable project—slum area health
care, rural schools, homes for refugees—even at the cost of
fueling inflationary pressures which are so dangerous to the
common welfare? When is it right, and when is it not right, to
resign? (Every Monday morning, according to some of the more
utopian Christian journalists: but what will happen to the power
you hand over?)

The strains on people like Bayard Rustin and Hubert Humphrey
during President Johnson's administration deserve careful examination, not slick condemnation. It is my conviction that Christians
in general, and radical Christians in particular, have a heavy obligation to understand and to respect the terrible strains under which
many politicians work and live. It is so easy to jeer.

Personal Pressures

However, political life is not all dramatic stands for justice, or
sinister deals with the FBI or with great corporations. It is clear
from many published memoirs that other temptations are as powerful, and perhaps more insidious. The strange life-style enforced
by the political routine produces many personal and spiritual problems, which Stewart Alsop and others have often described:[7] the
need to live in two or three places (it is invariably fatal to neglect
your home constituency), and the domestic and church rootless-
ness which often follows; the excruciating dullness and tedium of
the long hours of committees and debates (the great achievements
of a man like Jean Monnet, the background inspirer of the European Community, were interspersed with months and years of
plodding and waiting);[8] the spiritual loneliness which many have
commented on, notably Senator Mark Hatfield;[9] the continual
pressure to accept party policy, to fall in with the usual and sometimes degrading devices of political publicity and television cover-

age; and above all, the need to get elected and reelected (what use is a politician who is constantly a noble failure?).

The Call to Remember the Gospel

With such pressures it is easy to be "corrupted," to conform, to be no longer salt in the political arena, whether one's politics are conservative or radical, Democrat or Republican. Of course a Christian politician has to beware of resigning too often, of becoming Mr. Shining Armor, and thus never gaining promotion. Though I am certain that many church criticisms of politicians are insensitive and unfair, and though we must always acknowledge that many of our particular political opponents are sincere Christian people (no easy thing to do, for either conservatives or radicals, when it is something as bitter as the Vietnam War), we must also remember that the gospel calls us all to hard decisions, to a committed style of living, and to a constant preparedness not to conform. Christians in politics are no more exempt than the rest of us from a constant self-examination as to whether they are less sharp than they used to be in discerning good and evil, and less tough than in earlier days in taking personal and political risks for the Lord. The records of recent history seem to show that many good people in the political system took too long to speak out against Hitler or Stalin, against Joseph McCarthy, against the Vietnam War, against apartheid in South Africa. The art of knowing when to speak out, when to wait, and how to find allies to join in your protesting, is one of the finest skills which a politician can acquire. And some, through the weariness of office or the dreary loneliness of unpopular opposition, lose heart.

On this point we need to note some of the arguments advanced by Arthur Gish in his important book *The New Left and Christian Radicalism*. I cannot say that I agree with all his stances, but he is right when he warns against too easy an acceptance of the compromises and ambiguities which are the common currency of political life:

> It is one thing to talk of compromise in the sense of flexibility and co-operation, a willingness to live ambiguities of life, to be aware of

our questionable motives and imperfect actions, to reject dogmatism; and it is quite another thing to talk of selling out, retreating, being less than faithful, basing decisions on expediency rather than on faithfulness to one's commitment.[10]

How the Churches Can Help

What, in particular, can churches and church people do to affirm, to support, and to develop an intelligent critical dialogue with Christians who have committed themselves to political careers? I am sure that these three things are necessary: praise, prayer, and criticism (surely necessary but not first in priority). In the past, it has been a fine tradition in many churches that we pray for our "rulers," a tradition with strong New Testament roots and firmly established, for all kinds of reasons, by past European kings and princes. I suspect though, after a good deal of attending Sunday worship (in churches both of the more "established" and of the "sect" traditions), that this is rather too often a nominal and perfunctory part of the service, except perhaps during a major election campaign. It was continually distressing to me that, in a kind of collective spiritual amnesia, in so many United States churches which I visited on Sunday mornings very little time was spent in agonizing in prayer about the Vietnam War, or in thoughtful praying for the president and other political leaders and congressmen. This is not at all the same thing as sermons offering attacks on, or defenses of, American foreign policy. Again, not many clergy or congregations seem to develop the art of affirming the life and hard work of local politicians, state legislators, and congressmen and women from their particular districts, though they will readily pray for their bishop, their superintendent, or their church school organizers. We must learn to pray earnestly and with understanding, for our politicians, for their power and their problems.

In England, one or two communities of cloistered nuns devote much time to a study of the political news, and then to constant and informed intercession for those with political responsibility. If the prayer life of a congregation is to have strength and power, then one of its elements must be an intelligent reflection on the strengths and weaknesses of our democratic processes, and also on the strengths and weaknesses of our democratic politicians. Yes, the weaknesses. Though there is no doubt, especially in local congregations, that both clergy and laity, and in particular clergy, will do well to advance criticisms of politicians and political events with some sensitivity, it is the function of the church to prophesy, to proclaim the gospel, to offer both visions for the future and practical judgments for the present. The importance of laity programs in Europe, like the *Kirchentage* or the dialogues at some Swiss conference centers, is that they offer more than just amiable discussions and careful analyses of political and social problems; they do have some theological content, some biblical criticisms, some challenge to *change* things. The importance of some of the best congregations in Washington, D.C., is that—without a naive utopianism—in both the preaching and the parish discussion groups there is a careful Christian critique of political life. This work needs to be developed by clergy and by other Christian educators who understand the risks of speaking too simplistically and of being outside the convolutions of political bargaining, who learn how to develop honest and outspoken relationships with Christians in politics and how to make sharp critical points when this is necessary. I suspect that if some politicians are weary of church leaders who are always asking for impossible reforms (and at the same time for lower taxes), others most definitely want the church "to be the church," to stand for something more than conformity with present political shallowness, to set some goals for a much fairer and more just American and world society—provided that church leaders do not callously berate the politicians for living in the midst of compromises and ambiguities.

Sometimes, and for some Christians, both of the left and of the right, such an uneasy partnership between church and political leaders seems impossible and indeed a betrayal of sincerely held opinions. Not least among the tragedies of Latin America—Chile, Brazil, Bolivia—are the searing tensions which beset political leaders and revolutionaries, as well as both conservative and radical church leaders. The body of Christ is most bitterly divided. But in North America, at least, it should be possible for far more fruitful relationships to be developed between Christians who engage in the hard, frustrating, and yet peculiarly satisfying work of the democratic political process, and those who are prepared to work with them, not in isolation from them, in developing a strong and yet realistic proclaiming of where we stand under the judgment of the gospel.

7

Christian Business Executives

Our cows are not contented: they are always trying to do better.

Billboard, Denver, Colorado

Laypeople cannot be daily prophets.

GEORGE MORRISON

In the last fifty years, Christians active in business and industrial affairs have seen some considerable variations in the attitudes which church leaders have shown toward such activities. We need to disentangle these confusions, for they have been unusually productive of misunderstandings, and have often hampered open and fair dialogue between clergy, theologians, and business leaders. They have also often obstructed any understanding that Christians may actually rejoice that God has called them to a life of responsibility in corporations, great or small.

There are still relics of the old European prejudice against "trade" and business activity, a prejudice common among "gentlemen" (including those clergy who thought of themselves as gentlemen) in the nineteenth century and earlier. In the United States, such scruples often vanished before a simple admiration of the skills and power of important tycoons of "the age of enterprise," an approval sometimes helped, it must be admitted, by the munificent donations to churches, cathedrals, and religious charities which often followed the making of capitalist fortunes.

71

Irving Kristol has written of "businessmen as heroes" and there
are plenty of fulsome tributes to capitalistic enterprise in the sermons and religious books of pre-1914 America.

Things are very different nowadays, as Mr. Kristol rightly re-
marks, "Today businessmen, and especially corporate executives, are just about the only class of people which a television
drama will feel free to cast as pure villains."[1] A considerable
number of church leaders share in this general prejudice against
business people. Making a profit is strongly though imprecisely
suspect. On this point in particular it is surely necessary to work
out rather sharply just *what kinds of profits are and are not legitimate*. Somehow a career in business is seen as far less "worthy"
than "working with people," or in a nonprofit enterprise. Banking
and insurance might be regarded as moderately reputable jobs, but
in the strange hierarchy of occupations which underlies much
Christian thinking about society to be a bishop or a community
worker or even a teacher ranks high, while to be an executive in a
supermarket chain, a dealer in foreign currencies, or a manufac-
turer of television sets is something of which Christians ought
rather to be ashamed.

Before we can consider the real possibilities and temptations
which face Christians who are influential business people or corporate executives, we must get rid of this kind of nonsense. It is
possible to be a strict and dogmatic Christian socialist or anarchist,
and to maintain that either a totally state-dominated economy or a
system of village communes is the only kind of economic system
pleasing to God. It is possible, but I suspect that very few of even
the most radical Christians in North America actually maintain this
kind of theory consistently or expect that such a system can ever
be achieved. If in a country like Britain or the United States there
are to be major sectors of trade and industry which are neither
nationalized nor run, say, by cooperative enterprises, how can it
be maintained that it is an improper activity for Christians to take
part in private industry? Of course the precise definition of which
parts of the economic system are to be state run and which are to be
private (with no doubt many public supervisory controls) is one of

the greatest political debates of the twentieth century, and many Christians are sincerely divided about the details.

It needs to be said plainly and emphatically that in principle there is nothing against, and much for, Christian laity playing a major part in the power networks and structures of business enterprises. There is much fuzzy thinking among socially minded Christians about this issue, and this hinders the development of an intelligent discussion about how much state influence there *should* be in industry. Nor does such fuzzy thinking acknowledge the inevitable tensions in any style of economic organization. As British economist Denys Munby wrote some years ago:

> We need a Christian critique of any social system or method of economic organization. But equally clearly there is no "perfect Christian system," which all will be love and friendship, with no conflicts and clashes. Complex social systems are not families, and cannot be made into "happy families" by any sleight of the hand or over-all reorganization.[2]

Moreover, such thinking does not give any kind of affirmation to church people involved in business corporations that their work—hiring and firing, buying and selling, making profits and losses—can be genuinely useful to their fellow citizens and distinctly pleasing to Almighty God.

The Real Dilemmas

Christian business leaders today face enough genuine problems without having their commitment to their jobs sneered at. Some of these problems are common to all business executives, some are peculiar to those who acknowledge a Christian discipleship, some are personal and individual, some are intimately connected with the structure of today's commerce and industry.

There are many discussions in the management literature about the problems of a corporate executive's life-style; it is worthwhile outlining some of them here, for Christians do not always have much imaginative insight into other people's daily routines. Most pastors and professional people know something of the business person's problems with career mobility, and the ways in which those constant business trips can eat into family and neighborhood life, and into any deep involvement in local church life. Not so many, perhaps, understand the strong commitment to ambition, to drive, to performance which is demanded of a modern executive. Many religious teachers and preachers are a bit ambivalent about ambition anyway, though they may hesitate to exalt the unambitious too openly. It is certainly quite difficult for business leaders to value highly competence and achievement in sales or in management, while at the same time believing "it is not what you achieve, but what you are that matters." Another business virtue which is thought rather little of by church people is risk taking, which brings the possibility of real failure—not just a disappointment but loss of the job, premature retirement, or bankruptcy. Yet another business virtue is the need for constant innovation, constant competition, constant thinking of the future, not the past.

Of course many business leaders are not as sharp as this. They move comfortably from precedent to precedent, from Monday's routine to Saturday's leisure just as uneventfully as any civil servant or seminary professor. But wielding of real power and responsibility in business and industry demands aggressive, thrusting skills far removed from the rather bland neighborliness suggested in many Sunday sermons. As Professor Abraham Zaleznik has argued powerfully, "Frank recognition of the importance of personality factors, and a sensitive use of the strengths and limitations of people in decisions on power distributions can improve the quality of organizational life."[3]

Besides such personal problems, there are genuine questions of structural responsibilities which affect many business people. We have already pointed out the unfair, ill-defined, general condemnations of business life which float around in some church discussions and departments of social responsibility. However, just as in politics, there is a fair and important analysis to be made of the *possible* corruptions in business, especially in big business; just as it behooves a bishop to know about the possible evils in the denominational structures, so corporate executives have a clear duty to know what may in fact be going wrong with their corporation or industry, and what if anything can be done about it. There are not many business people as realistic as the famous Christian layman and industrialist J. Irwin Miller when he remarked, "I'm a businessman. I spend my time choosing between two wrongs, and being shot down for the one I choose."[4] What the acerbic, powerful critic C. Wright Mills has called "structural immorality"[5] is always a possibility in capitalistic enterprises as, of course, in all other types of economic systems. The rule for the Christian is: Everything is to be questioned; nothing is to be accepted or condemned without examination. If outside critics of industry sometimes abuse and condemn out of sheer prejudice or habit, too many leaders of industry have in the past assumed that all was well in their financial or industrial structures until confronted, too late, with a major scandal. Sometimes professional solidarity or even snobbery has helped to produce a climate of conservative probity and decent dealing (at least in the narrow sense), sometimes loyalty to a financial institution or to a major corporation has helped protect both shareholders and staff and customers from shabby treatment, but not always. Some time ago, Irving Kristol himself provided an interesting example of unfortunate corporate "clubbiness" which does not properly examine stock market practice, and complained:

"A number of these corporations then proceed to behave in such a way as to offend and outrage the corporation's natural constituency: the stockholders. More important, the business community as a whole remains strangely passive and silent before this spectacle. This disquieting silence speaks far more eloquently to the American people than the most elaborate public relations campaign. And it conveys precisely the wrong message.[6]

Very often it has only been such an article, a consumer organization, or a government—yes, a government agency—which has forced even the greatest firms, for example General Motors, into proper manufacturing and trading practices.

Christian business executives have first a duty to know, as far as possible, what is going on. They must then see what is possible for them and their allies to achieve within their own organization. They must also realize the limits of such voluntary self-regulation. If firm A pays better wages, carefully observes safety regulations, refuses to pay kickbacks, and so on, while firm B does not, then firm A may (not always, but quite often) go to the wall while firm B makes large profits. There almost always has to be some public or government supervision to make sure that both firm A and firm B obey satisfactory standards, and as we shall see, such public regulation of all firms in an industry conspicuously fails to work in international trade.

Are They Insulated from the Real World?

Let me also raise an important question of life-style, which today hangs in the background of many awkward discussions about corporate executives. By the nature of their lives, they tend to live busily but very comfortably. It is expected of them that they live in rather exclusive homes, that they enjoy excellent incomes and pensions. Without indulging in utopian egalitarianism and suggesting that they "sell all their goods," we must note that their wealth and life-style undoubtedly divides them from many of their fellow Christians, and it is likely that they may fall into what John Westergaard has called "a passive enjoyment of advantage and privilege." They may not so much consciously adopt, as gently slide into, extremely conventional and parental attitudes toward blacks, minorities, and many women employees. It is certainly the role of the church to jolt them out of complacency in such matters. In particular, in the 1980s there is need for a radical rethinking of the strains and opportunities which face Christian women executives employed in business firms.

Indeed, perhaps a modern version of the hard saying, "It is easier for a camel to go through the eye of a needle than for a rich man to enter into the kingdom of heaven," is "than for a busy, wealthy, corporation executive to enjoy real solidarity with Christians working for a just society." The difference between the assumptions of church leaders about the fairness of modern America or, say, of the Federal Republic of Germany and those of radical writers like Brian Wren and William Coats[7] is so great that church leaders, theologians, and parish clergy should be profoundly concerned to explore this phenomenon. What Coats has called "the sovereignty of inequality in the American system" seems natural enough to many business leaders, but a national disgrace to others concerned with the continuing poverty among many fellow United States citizens, let alone in the world outside North America.

The Multinationals

Such questions of business ethics come up with particular emphasis in the activities of multinational and transnational corporations, and there is rightly much concern about them. However, it is distressing that the leaders of such corporations are too often subject to what can only be described as vague generalized abuse. Even great and responsible Christian organizations like the World Council of Churches have sometimes indulged in rhetorical rather than thoughtful criticism of them. The "multis" have become the demonic powers of our time, and their leaders the evil villains of our modern world, denounced by Christian writers from Jacques Ellul to Charles Elliott. The old books on ethics used to ask: Is it possible for a prostitute or a barkeeper to be saved? Could one be a gambler and a Christian? Now one is more likely to ask the question about an international banker or a major leader in Shell or ITT, and when such Christians (often rather faithful members of their local congregations) appear occasionally at major church conferences on social responsibilities and the world economic order they are sometimes not only bitterly attacked, but also shunned like moral lepers. It was refreshing to find at the World Council of Churches conference in 1979 on Faith, Science and the Future one section protested against this kind of attitude and asked, pointedly, "Do men and women who lead or work in transnational corporations constitute a special type of being, with more unfavorable features than the rest of mankind?"[8]

In other, distinctly conservative, church circles, there is much more likely to be a general approval of such stalwarts of American capitalism, but again with little careful analysis of their considerable powers and responsibilities. I think, therefore, that it is worthwhile detailing how a careful and constructive criticism of Christians working in international business may be worked out.

It is commonplace to suggest that all business executives have
sixfold responsibilities: to their colleagues in leadership, their
shareholders, their employees, their government, their consumers
and the ordinary citizens of their country, and their families and
themselves. It is a sobering thought that international executives
(whether they work at the head office or at an overseas office) must
at least double these responsibilities and relationships, and it is
disturbing to read a number of reports from Christian organizations
working in this field (for instance the lay academy at Bad Boll near
Stuttgart, Germany) that very often business people are sent out
to foreign countries with no kind of thoughtful facing of these
questions.[9]

1. They have heavy responsibilities to their colleagues and
superiors at the head office. In actual fact, these are normally
expected to override all others. Nevertheless, they may also have
(especially if their own nationality is that of another country rather
than that of the head office) a strong feeling of loyalty to colleagues
in an overseas office. Such a shift in loyalty produces very complicated results in organizational frustrations and career patterns.

2. They have, of course, responsibilities to their parent company's shareholders. There may well also be local shareholders,
whose interests are not necessarily identical with those back
home. Indeed, a number of major multinational corporations, especially in the United States, so much dislike divided loyalties that
they try to avoid altogether having "joint ventures." Nevertheless, an overseas government may insist on them—for proper or
less-than-respectable reasons.

3. In multinational corporations there are complications in considering a manager's responsibilities to employees. It is often difficult
enough to remember the interests of home nationals. (How
long does one argue in Detroit for those unemployed in Tennessee,
or in London for those hurt by plant closures?) It is more difficult
still to consider the human problems of employees in Tanzania or
in Chile. Managers at the head office may very easily ignore them;
those working overseas may be equally callous, or not have
enough clout to influence corporate headquarters back in New

York or Toronto, or simply feel defeated by the conflicting claims of capital-intensive technology against local demands for the employment of as many unskilled people as possible.

4. To maintain relations with two distinct national governments may be equally complicated. Most major Western governments are now intimately concerned with multinational companies and their activities. There will be problems of taxation; for sometimes, at least (if not as often as is alleged), multinational corporations try to declare profits in low tax countries rather than to British or American tax authorities. There may be currency problems; the *Wall Street Journal* of 13 February 1973, reported on a U.S. government study which clearly indicated the power of multinational corporations to accentuate a currency crisis, even though it kindly suggested that they do not normally act in any wicked or predatory way. (It is extremely difficult to suggest that the leadership of a multinational company should not protect its currency holdings, say of pounds or dollars, as well as it legally can.)

There will be labor problems; the AFL-CIO is constantly pressing the U.S. administration to watch that "jobs are not exported" by attempts to use overseas labor at cheaper costs, including highly skilled labor—research and development can cost five times more to organize in the United States than in some European countries. There may be security problems; some industrial and technological secrets must not be spread around; some raw materials must be controlled as firmly as possible.

But multinational managers must also consider pressures from the governments of the countries in which their corporations operate. Even if the manager is in Dallas, there may be some pressure from an oil sheik or President Kaunda; if the manager is actually working overseas there may be constant daily pressure from a local government, and much suspicion as to what the head office and the home government are up to.

5. It is extremely important to remember that such pressures from governments do not, of course, necessarily represent the interest of citizens, especially the poorer citizens and national minorities. A Washington administration may or may not always

consider the best interests of minorities in the United States in its commercial diplomacy, and the same is true of European governments. It is equally clear that in an overseas country the government (whether "democratically elected" or not) may, often enough, take the side of either a tiny elite group, or a group of army officers, or a tribal power bloc. It is difficult enough for conscientious multinational executives to balance the demands of, say, the American and Liberian governments on them and their company; it is considerably more complicated for them to work out their responsibilities to United States and Liberian citizens. They may well be tempted not to try.

6. One's responsibilities to one's family and to oneself may be simpler, but there is ample evidence that working with a multinational company does produce additional family and personal strains. Even those who firmly stay in a New York or London head office can receive surprising criticisms these days from their friends or their children for working for "wicked" multinational corporations; those who go overseas, maybe just for relatively short periods, have considerable problems about their personal life-styles, education for the children, international friendships, and the like. And then there may be, especially for longer-term expatriates, the familiar problems of keeping up-to-date, or watching the promotion patterns and company intrigues back at the head office, or of finding a reasonable job and a new pattern of social life when the overseas tour is over.

So much for explanations. The situation is as complicated as this, and it is unfair and simplistic to pretend otherwise. It is equally wrong to suggest that because things are so complicated, the international business executive can avoid making persistent efforts to balance all these responsibilities. Too many still seem to assume that they must give overriding priority to their families, themselves, and their corporate head office, and that all the rest (even their home government, except in time of great emergency) must be adjusted to as easily and painlessly as possible. There is, I suggest, a special responsibility on top managers working at corporate headquarters to remember these extra dimensions of multinational capitalism. They have great power, if anyone has.

Control of the Multis

We must remember again the distinction between a corporation and a government, and insist that it is the proper function of governments to control and supervise financial and business firms. Sometimes overseas governments are quite powerful—for good or ill—even if their countries seem terribly small and vulnerable. A major difficulty here is that they have too often developed only one or two very powerful and clumsy weapons to use, such as the threat of expulsion or confiscation (as in Chile or Libya). These threats are real, for what American or European government will now send a gunboat or the marines to protect a multinational's plants or mines unless extremely strategic materials are involved? But such measures are drastic ones. Western governments are sometimes anxious, but more often reluctant, to develop adequate controls on their corporations working overseas (maybe for tax purposes). It is argued sometimes that if their regulatory powers are too severe, other corporations based elsewhere—perhaps Singapore, Beirut, or Lichtenstein—will simply take over business with less scrupulous supervision of their activities. There is something in this argument, but there has never been a thorough consideration of what the United States, Canadian, European Community, and Japanese governments might do if they acted together to set and enforce more adequate standards for international corporations.

Clearly what is needed is the development of some major international controls for multinational corporations. There are at the moment only the vaguest beginnings of such international law: the possibilities of international arbitration, the work of the International Chamber of Commerce, a few United Nations proposals. Equally, there is a need for some kind of international guild or association for multinational managers, with the beginnings of an international code of ethics, such as the airline pilots are beginning to achieve.

Despite all the difficulties in these "gray areas" for international business leaders, in the last resort we must be sharply critical of the ethical insensitivities shown by all too many of them. It has been particularly difficult to persuade leaders of multinational enterprises to understand the social and political implications of their commercial agreements. To quote J. Irwin Miller again, "Once a company has decided to enter [a country] it should commit itself to learning that country inside out."[10]

Those involved in international trade and finance have a special obligation to remember the poor, the wretched, and the oppressed in the countries they deal with, and where they make good profits. In fact, however, they often have every temptation to forget in their comfortable boardrooms in Frankfurt or Chicago or London. Even those who visit or work in places like Johannesburg or Santiago are extraordinarily insulated from the daily life of the ordinary people, as they are driven from comfortable homes or suburbs to the executive suites of plants or mines and then on to the country club for a little leisure.

They have a deep and continuous responsibility at least to seek the facts, even when these are very unpleasant, to take every opportunity to listen to ordinary employees and to local community leaders, and to see what freedom they do have to improve conditions overseas. There is now a good deal of evidence (for example in South Africa) that senior multinational executives can, and therefore should, achieve more than the very modest goals they tend to set themselves. As A. W. Clausen, president of the Bank of America, has ventured to write (to be fair, it is I think clear that he has tried to hold his immense financial institution to this goal): "Growing numbers of people believe it is the responsibility of the multinational firm to behave in such a way that the international political institutions it spawns will enhance personal liberty."[11]

8

Christian Labor Union Leaders

> When you're head of a union, you've got to be a sociologist, a marriage counselor, father confessor, psychiatrist, economist, legal expert, all wrapped into one. You must have the desire to help people help themselves.
>
> JOSEPH A. BEIRNE

> You can't get tomorrow's job with yesterday's skills.
>
> Slogan, New York subway trains

COMMITTED CHRISTIANS in the labor unions? As powerful leaders in the Auto Workers or the Mine Workers? The very idea is difficult for many middle-class church people to grasp. Indeed there seems recently to have been rather little public discussion about the role of the laity in the unions in America. This essay can only point to some of the questions to be considered.

The role of the unions in American society is not one which Christian churches have ever been easy about. Certainly the Roman Catholic Church showed, in the nineteenth and early twentieth centuries, much sympathy with the struggling immigrant workers and their attempts to gain better working and living conditions. I suspect that some of the Catholic willingness to support early union leaders (so long as they were not antireligious socialists) needs to be more generally recognized as something of a counterbalance to the notorious Protestant pro-employer and anti-union bias, which was so strong at least up to World War II, and is certainly not dead yet among some Protestant and Evangelical church people. A rather forgotten book by Jerome Davis, *Labour Speaks for Itself on Religion,* published way back in 1929,[1] gives a damning impression about the alienation of the labor movement from most of the organized Christian churches. It must be admitted that the contributors are particularly severe in condemning the anti-union utterances of clergy; perhaps they assumed that the laity would be even less favorable to their cause. As James Simpson, then secretary of the Canadian Labour Party, wrote:

> Labour thinks the church is insincere. It believes the ministers of the Gospel are less inclined to make a central sacrifice for the advancement of their cause than the leaders of the Labour Movement are compelled to make because of the injustice of those who uphold the Church. They have vivid recollections of the dismissal of men from industries operated by so-called Christians, because they exercised the right to organise for their own protection and advancement.[2]

As late as May 1953, David S. Burgess wrote in the *Christian Century,* "We are criticized without sympathy and reviled without understanding."

In fact, by the 1950s, the situation so far as the more liberal main-line churches were concerned was fast improving. The massive National Council of Churches' series on The Churches and Economic Life included a volume by John A. Fitch[3] which was sensibly sympathetic toward many aspects of labor union work, while acknowledging some of the abuses to be found in many of them. We must recall that in the 1950s and 1960s the then powerful department of Church and Economic Life at the National Council of Churches, under the exceptional leadership of C. Arild Olsen (who had many links with both government and union leaders), did much in the immediate post–Joseph McCarthy era to promote a general appreciation of and strong personal links with important union presidents. Such work was paralleled by several denominational departments of church and society though it must be admitted that it was not easily accepted by many laity in the pews and in corporation offices, especially in the South and Southwest.

Churches Against the Unions?

Since 1960 many senior church leaders, even in the most liberal denominations, seem to have turned anti-union. It is not only a matter of the clear and well-publicized corruption in some major unions, like the Teamsters. There has also been a strong feeling (not always well-documented) that the unions are now more likely to be a dangerous labor monopoly than a force for social reform, and that they are a major obstacle to the advancement of blacks, Chicanos, and other minorities. The confrontation between the Teamsters and the United Farm Workers was a considerable factor in developing church opinion, especially as some important Roman Catholic and Protestant clergy and laity were and are deeply committed to Cesar Chavez. There were also frequent tensions between church community workers and union organizations, with sometimes little attempt to understand the deep ethnic and local roots of union history.[4] There is no doubt that union leaders and their members (just like many suburban white congregations) are often prejudiced against open housing, the advancement of women to higher paid jobs, and similar causes. Indeed, the suspicion of the unions among liberal and radical Christians sometimes almost brings these liberal Christians into an unholy alliance with deeply conservative and old-fashioned capitalist church members, who simply want to keep unions out of church hospitals and church day schools.

Nevertheless, there are many sincere members of the body of Christ in positions of union leadership and surely we have the responsibility to understand before we judge, whether we feel sympathetic toward union activities or whether we feel that something has gone badly wrong with at least some American and Canadian unions. I am afraid we must be rather ashamed of the sheer lack of knowledge about union organization and union management which is evident among many church people, even those who are concerned with social relationships and social evils.

The Troubles of Union Leaders

In the first place, we must realize that though a small minority of union leaders have adopted a life-style and accepted incomes which are excessive by any standards of solidarity with ordinary people, such incomes and expense accounts are still very much the exception rather than the rule (much more exceptional than among major corporation executives). It has been reckoned that there are about twenty presidents of major international corporations with very large incomes and perquisites to match: there are many union leaders, often with responsibilities equal to those of major business leaders, who live quite modestly. Of course there has been for many years corruption at the top of several major unions—that in the Teamsters Union has been well publicized recently, especially by Steven Brill.[5] What is valuable about his book, and what should be studied by church people, is the wide spectrum of leadership styles and personal ambitions indicated in his stories of different Teamster leaders, and in particular, the personal tragedy of Harold Gibbons, who might have produced a union leadership so different from that of James Hoffa or Frank Fitzsimmons. To condemn the Teamsters (2.5 million members) as totally corrupt is as simplistic as to condemn Episcopalians as dissolute on the basis of clergy divorces in California.

There are many other causes besides corrupt power struggles for the difficulties in the great American unions as they try to face the 1980s. Some of them have been very well listed in the admirable Rockefeller Brothers Fund study, *Labor and the American Community*.[6] Unions are in deep trouble as bureaucracies. Their leaders tend to be elderly, in the past very skilled at local elections and organization (so dependent on ethnic and neighborhood links), but now lacking management and planning skills, frequently overworked (and bad at delegation), sometimes "burned out" after appalling long hours of tedious work year after year. They often feel not only inadequate to face the very difficult technological changes threatening their members but also are secretly afraid of able younger people who might show them up—not only on the other side of the bargaining table but also among their own membership. J. B. S. Hardman has gone so far as to write of the "intellectual poverty" among union leadership.[7] Such union presidents and executives are not easily going to hold constructive discussions with business school experts, university sociologists, or church intellectuals.

They are likely to be particularly defensive about the pace of technological progress, of what A. H. Raskin has called "the big squeeze on labor unions."[8] This is not at all a philosophical skepticism about innovation, but a lurking background fear that technologists are, now more than ever, enabling corporations to replace people by machines, and that the next fifty years will see quite massive unemployment because of computer technology and the increasing pace of automation (which the British call "chips with everything" since the new devices are cheap as well as clever). Very often, both in America and in Europe, unions are strong enough to protect their members against layoffs and redundancies *for one generation,* but not for longer. Men and women may not now be fired in the ruthless style of the past, but they are not replaced when they retire. Unemployment, underemployment, and increased leisure are exactly the kind of topics on which union leadership in the United States must now concentrate; they are not yet as ruthless and realistic about the future as the radical British trade union writers Clive Jenkins and Barrie Sherman, who have simply called their new book *The Collapse of Work.*[9] Church thinkers can very helpfully join in discussion of these topics (as they have often done in the European laity centers in recent years). They have to understand, however, the dull sourness of automation for many union people, and the strong tensions developing among the younger generation of union leaders, such as the more openly socialist ideas from leaders like William W. Winpisinger of the International Association of Machinists and Aerospace Workers.[10]

We must recognize also the psychological and class tensions between many union leaders and white-collar reformers. I recommend rather strongly two recent reports which seem to me to get to

the heart of some of these differences: William Kornblum's *Blue
Collar Community* about South-Side Chicago and Robert
Schrank's *Ten Thousand Working Days,* detailing his remarkable
pilgrimage through many jobs, including that of a union official[11]
are important reminders of the remaining class differences between blue-collar and white-collar citizens. These differences,
more often than we like to accept, divide even senior union executives from church leaders. As Kornblum writes, "The institutions
of the South Side (including the local Catholic churches) demand
an endless series of exceptions to the formalities of middle class
legality."[12] Suburban Protestants have sometimes almost no idea
of the way in which blue-collar people live, survive, and thrive with
quite different personal and community ethics to those of middle-
class congregations. The very language with which many powerful
union leaders condemn what they consider "limousine liberals"
can indicate something of the difficulties of establishing what
a theologian might call meaningful and constructive dialogue
with them.

A New Start Is Possible

Can church leaders now make a new effort to develop useful
relationships with union leaders, and especially with those of them
who are practicing Christians? Can the Roman Catholic Church, in
particular, now revive its past connections with the unions? It is
extraordinary how many such Catholic links, strong even up to the
1950s, have faded away, and indeed Patrick J. Sullivan recently felt
he must insist that "religious leaders not be caught up in the effort
to destroy unions."[13] It has been very encouraging to read reports
of the Washington, D.C., conference in June 1979, designed to
develop again more positive contacts between Catholics and union
leaders. It is clear that such experienced social-action organizers
as Monsignor John Egan and Monsignor George Higgins are determined to develop these new initiatives. As Monsignor Higgins
has written:

> Experience has taught me to restrain my enthusiasm about meetings
> of this type. Yet I am reasonably optimistic about this one. It was a

significant step in the right direction, and I fully expect it to result in a modest but potentially important church-labor network within two or three years. The sooner the better.[14]

I wish that such developments could be more fundamentally ecumenical, and that Protestant denominations were as eager to understand the powers and the difficulties of the leaders of America's great labor unions.

The veteran ecumenical leader Cameron P. Hall, who worked together with Arild Olsen at the National Council of Churches, has recently analyzed some of the common goals of church social-action departments and of the AFL-CIO, and shows that there is much mutuality between them; but his lead does not seem to have been followed up very energetically.[15]

I believe that Christian labor union executives have lost much because they are often marginal to the church to which they nominally belong. I suspect that we have never assessed how much Christian social-action thinking has suffered in the last ten years because it has been rather too much a matter of clergy and academics and environmentalists. It needs not only the realism and experience of political and business leaders, but also that which union leaders can bring from their tough industrial experience.

Dr. Cameron Hall has also related a fine story of a visit to the United States by Dr. Eberhard Müller, founder of the German lay academy at Bad Boll and inspirer of so much in European Christian thinking about the church and industrial life. Dr. Müller arrived at a time when there was major publicity about troubles in the Teamsters Union, and he was asked what should be done about this national scandal. Dr. Müller answered, "The church should bring together, across the country, Teamsters to discuss their own responsibilities towards the critical problems of their union." Dr. Hall comments, "I can still feel the impact-shock of that proposal. It was so simple and commonsensical, cutting right through to where the problem and its ultimate solution lay. At the same time how completely removed it was from anything that was on the minds of churchpeople."[16]

We do not need to be romantic about the abilities of the

Teamsters or of any other industrial group to achieve their own reforms to see that without dialogue with their leaders, and especially with those Christians who have responsible positions in their organizations, church thinking about unions will simply remain thin and ineffective.

9

Christian Leaders in the Police and the Military

> The Army also resembles the medieval church, pre-serving what every good officer believes to be "the true American virtues" in the midst of a decadent temporal society riven by disillusion and despair.
>
> LEWIS H. LAPHAM

> Where human institutions are concerned, love without criticism brings stagnation, and criticism without love brings destruction.
>
> JOHN W. GARDNER, *Recovery of Confidence*

It WOULD BE ridiculous to consider the problems of Christians wielding secular power in America without looking at those with responsibilities in the police and the military establishments. The senior officers of the FBI, the chiefs of the major state and urban police forces, the leaders of the armed forces and of the CIA; these are clearly and even notoriously people with power. Even in Roman Catholic circles, however, there seems at the moment to be little thoughtful examination of their work and their duties, as we look beyond the controversies and miseries of the past two decades and examine the role in the immediate future of American democracy.

The Police

Even when it comes to the police, who have an obvious role to play in the protection of citizens, particularly those who live in the inner cities, it is difficult to find careful and thorough assessments of their position today. I think there are two main reasons for this. One is the dismay and the disgust felt by so many liberal and radical Christians over police involvement in the events of the 1960s and 1970s, the struggles over civil rights, the urban ghetto riots, the agitation to end the Vietnam War, and the abuses of the Nixon administration. All these have seemed to put both the FBI and many local police administrations in an adversary relationship with the general populace, in which arguments and rhetoric on both sides planted long-term prejudices which are now very difficult to correct. As Albert J. Reiss, Jr., comments, "American society is more inhospitable towards its police than most societies."[1] Indeed, especially among middle-class, liberally minded Christian laity, there seems little understanding of the way in which police systems operate, and what is wrong and what is right in them. (I have the feeling that many clergy—both Protestant and Roman Catholic—do rather better understand than the laity not only the ambiguities but also the tough, "gray," rather grubby milieu in which inevitably most urban police systems must operate.) There are many vague church denunciations of "police brutality," "corrupt police," "the radical-right dominated FBI," and so on; there has not, I suggest, been a sufficiently careful examination as to *why* American police systems and police leaders are the way they are, what actually makes the difference between an acceptable and an unacceptable local force (there are enormous variations among the 40,000 police systems in the country), and what can be done to improve the worst and the mediocre agencies.

There are some excellent secular studies on police organization and police behavior to help in such assessments. Outstanding work has been published by James F. Ahern and by Albert J. Reiss, Jr. (Two works are cited in the notes for this chapter.) The writings of Ahern are especially valuable, because he came up through the ranks to be the police chief of New Haven, Connecticut, under the reforming administrations of Mayor Richard Lee; since he left that job he has been conspicuously, but responsibly, frank in his comments on police work. He is devastating about the frustrations which erode the best ambitions of police officers, from the moment they enter an urban force to the rare occasions when they reach a position of major responsibility. With the help of his experiences, and other careful criticisms of police systems today, I think we can identify some major areas to be considered in discussions about the future of police power in America and about the role of police leaders in developing reforms.

1. Most police chiefs are subject to strong, almost irresistible political pressures. These may occasionally be helpful as briefly with Richard Lee in New Haven and—more controversially—with Mayor Daley and Olando W. Wilson in Chicago. They may often be bitterly crippling on matters of major crime and major police deficiencies. There are many instances of state or city officials interfering with the pursuit of criminals, whether white-collar or mafia or gambling or drug rings. There are many recorded instances of police budgets being biased toward middle-class areas and against the inner city, and of necessary recruitment and supplies (in particular for adequate police training) being denied year after year. As Ahern writes, often enough "the stage is set for politicians to paralyze police if they are good and control them if they are not."[2]

2. Many police leaders have never been able to develop true professional competence, equivalent to the kind of senior management skills which people with similar budgets and power in business expect to achieve almost automatically in the development of their careers. It is not evident that the semimilitary styles of command, first giving and then expecting unquestioned obedience, are traditions which themselves ought to be accepted without question. Long years in the ranks very often reinforce blue-collar stereotypes and prejudices against blacks and other minorities, so that it is assumed that black areas will be areas with insoluble problems, where it is a waste of time to put the most capable officers (a point noted by many commentators, especially the Kerner Commission), and that it is impossible to find black

officers for promotion or white officers who will accept them. There are few opportunities for transfer to or from any other force, so that one is caught in the pressures of the peer group and the force's traditions until a pension is drawn (that may be forfeit for "difficult" behavior even for a quite senior officer). There is not much help from the professional association (The International Association of Chiefs of Police—actually 95 percent American in membership). All these factors militate against any persistent determination to improve one's own management capabilities or those of one's colleagues and assistants. What is frankly admirable is that many police chiefs and senior officers, nevertheless, do what they can despite every encouragement toward apathy and inertia.

3. We need a more realistic and thoughtful assessment of what can only be called "the limits of spying" by police agencies, and by federal agencies like the FBI. Church people need to recognize the need, even in the most liberal and democratic society, for some considerable police powers for the surveillance of suspected criminals and terrorists. Sometimes the comments of church people on the work of, for instance, the FBI or the federal drug agencies have been both innocent and ambiguous. The use of the FBI against those who protested the Vietnam War was justifiably attacked, but what of its activities against the Ku Klux Klan? Some of the work of the FBI needs to be affirmed by Christians, and we need a careful assessment of the proper activities of the considerable number of federal agents, both for the protection of citizens and for the help of the agencies themselves. We must move beyond wild assertions that "The United States is a fascist police state" and that kind of rhetoric.

4. The role of the press is crucial in matters of police abuse and corruption, and many journalists are skilled and heroic at uncovering scandals and resisting strong pressures to remain silent. Nevertheless, television and the newspapers live on scandals and atrocities, not on good news; it takes a very fine journalist to give sufficient credit to and to ensure proper publicity for police departments that do well.

5. The apathy of the general public, including church people, is terrifying. As James Ahern pointed out way back in 1973, the

arguments about the police in the 1960s soon gave way to a "withering of public interest." Apart from some understandable, but not well worked-out, demands for community police in some inner-city areas, many Christian people either just hope that they and their children won't get involved with the police, or seem to cover all police leaders, good, bad, or indifferent, with a blanket condemnation of the "system." Those who are committed to careers in police forces, either national or local, deserve better than this from us. As Ahern rightly comments, "We must realize our monumental obligation to those who have stayed in police work, who have 'kept the faith' while working at impossible jobs under absurd conditions."[3]

The Military

We cannot pretend that church people have any better record in their attempts to understand the position of their fellow Christians who hold positions of responsibility in the armed forces. There has been a great deal of discussion about disarmament and about just and unjust wars, but not enough about the dilemmas of people in the great military organizations—except perhaps, for the important question of conscientious objectors. It is clear that many senior officers in the military hold Christian beliefs; it is equally clear that they have almost no dialogue with the leadership of the main-line denominations on questions of war and peace, and of the proper role of the armed forces in a democratic society. There are several reasons for this serious lack of common argument.

In the first place, there is, of course, a most honorable tradition of pacifism among some Christians—Quakers and Mennonites, for example. There is also a less well thought-out romanticism about pacifism in a good many liberal clergy, on the lines: "We ought to be for peace; perhaps we have to have some armed forces, but let's not think too much about them." Very few clergy and even fewer laity seem to have established for themselves a careful theology of pacifism or of *limited endorsement* of some use of armed force at some times. The miseries of the Vietnam War, the gross excesses of the CIA, the almost ritual denunciations of the "military-industrial complex" (easier to attack than to analyze), the vague feelings that Jesus Christ could never have been a marine: all these have obstructed any serious communication between civilian and military Christians, and the armed-forces chaplains (perhaps especially the Protestant ones?) seem rather helpless here. This weakness in hard thinking about the role and the power of the military has been particularly serious in the grave days of the Iranian and Afghanistan crises, and of the threat of a major escalation in arms with the Soviet Union.

Here, as I see them, are some of the topics which need to be explored.

1. If the United States is to have armed forces (who, except for extreme pacifists, would really deny this?), what is their proper role in a reasonably democratic society, and what is their proper size?

2. John Kenneth Galbraith has insisted in an important but now rather neglected book, *How to Control the Military,* that it is *not* a question of military dishonesty or conspiracy, but rather one of the extraordinary military bureaucracy which has developed since 1939. He writes:

> the notion of a conspiracy to enrich and corrupt is gravely damaging to an understanding of the military power . . . the reality is far less dramatic and far more difficult of solution. The reality is a complex of organizations pursuing their sometimes diverse but general common goals. The participants in the organizations are mostly honest men whose public and private behavior would withstand public scrutiny as well as most.[4]

We know that all bureaucracies (even church bureaucracies) can impede necessary reforms and produce great injustices. What are the special difficulties and opportunities of controlling and reforming the military bureaucracy?

3. In particular, what are the right relationships between the military and the federal government, and Congress, and the courts? It is on record that recent presidents have exerted enormous influence on the armed forces, and that Congress has often approved vast military expenditures without careful debate. (The role of the Armed Services and Appropriations Committees and their composition require careful attention.)

4. The separateness of the military from civilian life and think-

ing, which has been thoughtfully explored by Lewis H. Lapham, has often produced what he calls a "military theology" among Army leaders.[5] He stresses the thorough education and training processes of the armed forces, the fostering of myths about communist conspiracies, and unpatriotic liberal clergy and do-gooders (which hamper a true assessment of communist power today). These influences produce a different kind of American citizen than the civilian "outside" the military world.

5. The failures and the excesses of the Vietnam War have greatly increased this separation from civilian life and from civilian Christians. Many military officers are now dogged, withdrawn, and even sullen as they continue with their daily routines. They feel (I think with some reason) that the military are now overly discredited and that their proper role in the maintenance of world peace is often ignored. Galbraith suggests that a proper movement to control the military establishment should take the line:

> This is not an anti-military crusade. Generals and admirals, and soldiers, sailors, and airmen are not the object of attack. The purpose is to return the military establishment to its traditional position in the American political system. . . . Whatever its moral case, there is no political future in unilateral disarmament.[6]

At the moment many senior military leaders feel personally despised, and would argue that their forces are the object of vague utopian attacks which, if they were successful, would bring the United States (and indeed Western Europe) into great danger.

6. Both Christians in the military and Christians in civilian life need to argue through again the wrong and the right kinds of patriotism: those which lead to an intolerant, often racialistic nationalism, and those which are a perfectly proper kind of loyalty for Christians to accept and to foster. Peter L. Berger has very helpfully developed some of the arguments, from his European as well as his American background, and he goes so far as to say: "The denigration of patriotism in important milieus of American intellectual and academic life today is dangerous."[7] Of course he in no way endorses the kinds of radical-right "patriotism" popular among a small minority of military leaders, who are themselves a disgrace to American democratic traditions.

7. The almost unbelievable role of modern science and technology in military and defense matters needs constant and careful public debate. Of course some details have to remain secret, but the intimate connection between some kinds of scientific research and military requirements needs a great deal of examination, not just denunciation.

8. In the same way that there is a need for something like the FBI, and other federal antidrug and antismuggling agencies, there is, of course, a need for some kind of American spy and antispy organization; anyone who suggests that this is not so simply has not reckoned with the sordid realities of international relationships in the modern world. This is not in any way to suggest that the activities of the CIA since 1945 have all been proper or justifiable: it is simply to say that some of its work has been absolutely essential to American defense. Indeed, in view of the disarray which has been evident in the organization of the CIA in the last few years, it is greatly to be hoped that somewhere in its overgrown bureaucracy, or somewhere else hidden in various security agencies, some people have continued to work quietly and very efficiently indeed on the primary tasks of spy and counterspy activities. Here, once again, we are in the world of ambiguities and compromises and unpleasant moral decisions, often much more messy and dirty than even the most exciting paperback thriller. (The novels of John Le Carré are outstanding in reflecting many of these moral dilemmas. See, for example, his *Spy Who Came In from the Cold* and *Smiley's People.*[8])

Church people must reflect now and then, that their safety depends and has to depend, in a corrupt world, on such people and their activities. They were heroes in World War II; they are much discredited today: we shall probably never know who promoted, who acquiesced in, and who tried in secret to protest against the abuses of CIA power in the last twenty years. But Christians must surely think of them and pray for them now and then, for their dirty work sometimes keeps us all safe.

10

Christians and the Power
of the Media

Good news shall travel fast.

Advertisement, British Columbia
Telephone Company

I don't give instant answers. Not to be thoughtful is to
be promiscuous.

NORTON SIMON

ALTHOUGH THIS BOOK is not intended to deal primarily with
questions of intellectual and cultural power, it really is not sensible
to omit from it some consideration of Christians working in the
communications media of the modern world, and especially in
television and in news journalism. Their intellectual gifts and
strengths are so intertwined with political and financial power
today that both government and major corporations are intimately
concerned with influencing what appears on television screens and
on the front pages of our daily papers; it is clear that those working
in, or controlling in any way, television or the press are often in
particularly ambiguous situations and under great pressure.

Indeed when it comes to television not a few modern commentators have considered that the right thing for Christians to do is to
avoid it as far as possible. British television performer Malcolm
Muggeridge has actually proclaimed in public that he got rid of his

television set, and has maintained that we should avoid the pernicious influence of the little box just "as early Christians kept away from the [Roman] Games."

Muggeridge repeats this blanket condemnation of television rather frequently, largely because he considers television-watching brainwashes people. In his London lectures, *Christ and the Media,* he was extremely harsh on the fantasy world of most television, and it is startling to consider that this extreme opinion has come to him largely through a study of British programs.[1] What he must think if he sees much American television must surely drive him to even more extravagant language.

Another recent critic, Jerry Mander, has produced an equally severe but far better thought-out condemnation in his *Four Arguments for the Elimination of Television,* a utopian tract which is nevertheless well worth critical attention.[2] Other writers, anxious to reform rather than to abolish so powerful a medium of communication, have concentrated not only on the extraordinary emphasis on violence, even in children's programs, but also on the fundamental commercialization of American television. In his *The Sponsor: Notes on a Modern Potentate,* Erik Barnouw, a veteran analyst of the industry, writes bitterly about the pernicious pervasiveness of so much selling, and of so much dependence on the Nielsen ratings and the sponsors' and advertisers' payments for programs.[3] John Kenneth Galbraith has indeed suggested that the whole United States consumer industry would collapse without the use of television advertising, and a figure as high as 4.5 billion dollars has been stated for the television advertisement industry.

This selling style spreads. In Britain the acceptance of advertisements on the independent channels (that is, the commercially owned television stations) not only affects all their program planning because of the demand for high ratings, but has also seriously influenced the British Broadcasting Corporation, whose leaders claim that they must match independent stations with equally popular programs, or they will lose their viewing audience altogether. The same tendency can be seen far too frequently in the American Public Broadcasting System which "advertises" its own future programs and leads into even serious discussions with exactly the same gimmicks as the commercial stations.

Supporting Christians in the Media

It may be of some slight comfort to those Christians working in television and similarly "pernicious" media that the extreme suggestion—believers should boycott such media—has not found very much support outside the more puritan sects. (Indeed it is significant how many Protestant evangelicals calmly accept for themselves and their children television programs which transgress many of their traditional moral standards.) At the London lectures given by Malcolm Muggeridge (published in *Christ and the Media*), Sir Charles Curran of the BBC and several of his colleagues firmly insisted that they were not ashamed to be working in television.

Albert van den Heuvel, formerly in charge of the communications department at the World Council of Churches and later General Secretary of the Dutch Reformed Church in the Netherlands, has insisted that it is a sign of loss of nerve in Christians to ignore the importance of the mass media today, for the mass media in many ways show a very great potential for the enlightenment and entertainment of modern man. He writes, "The media have no more inherent evil possibilities than any other thing man has invented."[4] Obviously they can be perverted, but in many ways they may be claimed for good. Van den Heuvel does admit that people have not looked sufficiently at the *structures* of the television industry. Clearly there are possibilities of corruption, and in particular of ignoring the interests of the poor, since they are not good consumers.

If we are to follow van den Heuvel and try to work out the great potential of working in the media, if in the phrase of John Lang of the BBC we are to offer a "word of encouragement" to those Christians who enter such careers, then certainly we have to try to assess the particular dangers which they may face. In the first place, it is undoubtedly true that almost all the media industries— television, films, newspapers, magazines, and advertising—provide a particularly heady, glittering, and glamourous atmosphere for young recruits. The informality, the superficial friendliness, the rushed schedules of an organization like network television can be a kind of trap in themselves, and can very much encourage young writers and producers to suspend their critical judgments.

To this must be added a particularly unfortunate flavor of hypocrisy about much of the so-called ethics of the media. There are carefully argued advertising codes for television, regulations about the portrayal of sex and violence in films, and cautious attitudes toward religious questions, but these can never be taken at their face value. As Douglass Cater has pointed out, a "few ghettoes of do-goodism" are allowed—but of course they must not occur in prime time. The desperate search for high figures, both in Britain and in the United States, for television or film audiences or for newspaper sales, works very heavily against thoughtful work. Even the style of weekly magazines is constantly under threat. Carll Tucker, the editor of *Saturday Review,* has emphasized the heavy pressures to make magazines always more glamourous, slicker, and more attractive to advertisers.[5]

Good News Is Not News

Such tendencies are of course particularly evident in the news and documentary programs. We must recognize how very many communities, particularly in rural areas, have had their moral horizons broadened by seeing national and international network news; Richard Nixon was perfectly correct in his assessment of the importance of television news in raising American consciousness both about the Vietnam War and about the Watergate scandals. Nevertheless, anybody working in television or on a daily newspaper knows the dreadful rule that *good news is not news: bad news is news.* Violence and disaster are news. The result can be a concentration of gloom and doom every morning and every evening. Sometimes this produces a strong reaction in the viewers and the readers. Byron Shafer and Richard Larson have suggested that frequent scenes of urban riots, muggings, and similar violence have been significantly important in developing right-wing "law and order" prejudices.[6] At other times such a predominance of dreary, depressing information and opinion just produces cynical and callous reactions from the general public.

No less a publicist than J. William Fulbright, who has often found the media a great help in his political campaigns, has written, "The national press would do well to reconsider its priorities. It has excelled in exposing wrongdoers, in alerting the public to the high crimes and peccadilloes of persons in high places. But it has fallen short—far short—in its higher responsibility of public education."[7]

It is also clear that brief snippets of news and simplistic judgments are a particular corruption of human intelligence. Jack Richardson has gone so far as to label the evening television news "six o'clock prayers," suggesting that the smooth compression of a day's events into the news bulletins and commentaries is more a civic religious ceremony than anything else.[8] It is depressing sometimes to meet good Christian people who have compromised not so much their moral standards as their intellectual integrity and their considerable skill in making thoughtful moral judgments because of the slick and glossy way in which they have to produce material for television or for the more superficial newspapers and weeklies. Of course there have to be popularizations in any kind of educational information system, but the dangers of simplistic distortions or of a dehumanizing blandness seem to be growing all the time. Leonard Woolf perceptively analyzed the temptations of daily or even some weekly journalism which "corrodes and erodes the editorial mind," so that the "scale of time against which you think of a revolution in Bulgaria or John Donne or Hitler's Nuremberg Laws or the behavior of the crowd at the Derby is five or at most seven days."[9] In television it may be only twenty-four hours.

Affirming and Intelligently Criticizing

We need to honor those good people who wrestle with these temptations and trends day by day. Those good people do, as Fred Friendly has said, operate in a "perpetual state of war with 'them.'" We need to look at the ways in which it is possible to stay in a responsible compromise: how to work in what are undoubtedly difficult jobs and still keep a sensitively critical faculty about the influence of the media. The recent studies of the World Association of Christian Communication on the ethical training of journalists need to be better known than they are.[10]

In looking at questions of power it is always a good rule to remember that one cannot rely solely on even the good and informed consciences of the people exercising authority and controlling finance, staffs, and projects. There always need to be outside checks and criticisms. Often, as with business corporations, such checks have to be governmental; even the strongest advocate of private enterprise will nowadays accept the need for pure food laws and checks on the safety of automobiles. When it comes to abuses in television and the press, there are special limits to the controls governments can and should and are likely to enforce. As we have seen rather frequently in recent years, the administration in Washington has not exactly acted as an Olympian judge impartially ruling on television and press abuses. It has been intimately, sometimes desperately and corruptly, involved in these abuses itself. The recent disclosures from the Commission on Federal Paperwork about the enormous amount of money which the federal government and its agencies spend on favorable publicity and the release of information are not reassuring on these points. In other countries it is notorious that government censorship and manipulation of the media is far more of a threat to the citizenry than even the strongest commercial pressures on freedom of opinion. We simply cannot trust governments to act as watchdogs over the media. Though sometimes they legislate wisely and, for instance, help the PBS or BBC networks to survive, often they seek to exert pressure on news commentators and to keep opposition critics off the air.

Here, overwhelmingly, there is a need for churches and church people (and for Christians in the media too) to encourage and to support those independent critics who constantly watch for possible abuses and praise real achievements. The old distinction between critics who "disturb and stimulate" as against those who simply "disturb and depress" is relevant here; it is unfortunate that in the United States there has, so far, been far less thoughtful critical writing about television than there has been about the film industry. Christian people in the United States need to be aware of the enormously good work done by some specialist critics, and in particular the work of publications, like the *Columbia Journalism Review,* which deal both with print media and television. In Britain, there never is any shortage of church attacks on the portrayal of sex and violence on television; there might be a little more appreciation of how people in the BBC and in the independent television companies are trying to achieve reasonable standards in programs, despite the heavy pressures of advertisers and of BBC bureaucrats concerned about the ratings before anything else.

There is also here an extraordinary responsibility laid on the general body of American church people. Some 60 percent of American citizens are apparently rather regular church members and attenders. Such an enormous number of people (ca. 130 million), almost all regular television viewers, radio listeners, and newspaper and magazine readers, must affect considerably the Nielsen ratings and circulation figures which the commercial owners of the media so much respect and watch. However, except for an occasional protest against exceptional violence or pornography, and for a little Roman Catholic pressure from time to time (now less common than even ten years ago), the churches have done rather little to educate their members in how to discriminate, how to pick and choose television programs in anything more than a crudely moralistic way. The writings of Michael J. Arlen and the maverick denunciations of the former Commissioner of the Federal Communications Commission, Nicholas Johnson, are of great importance here, and the experiments in Television Awareness Training, sponsored by a number of Christian denominations, need wider support.[11]

On adults, and overwhelmingly on children, television is a disturbingly powerful influence in developing political, cultural, and consumerist attitudes. Those inside the industry who know not only its dangers and its shallowness, but also its potential for good, need the prayers and the support as well as the intelligent criticisms which church groups should learn to develop and to make public. Lobbying the media giants is an art in itself, which should not be left to political or religious extremists.

11

Powerful Laity and the
Institutional Churches

> The Church must first, in real solidarity with the
> world, listen closely to what is actually going on in
> this world—which is loved by God.
>
> ADRIAAN VAN BIEMEN

> In reality the whole Christian life is conversion.
>
> YVES CONGAR, *Priest and Layman*

IT IS EVIDENT that the present relationships between responsible
and "strong" laity, as described in this book, and the institutional
churches are often not entirely satisfactory. This is particularly
true in Britain, where, in the old phrase, many of them "like to
have a church to stay away from," but it is also increasingly the
case in North America—perhaps especially in Canada. Where
such laity do, for reasons of loyalty or family or peer group pressures, turn up most Sunday mornings, it is not uncommonly a
matter of convention, of form, or of accepting church membership
as part of their lives, a part of residential suburbanism, and of
inculcating personal and family values—nothing much to do with
Monday's work.

This is a serious flaw in the development of the body of Christ.
Whether such laity vote with their feet or with their minds on
Sunday mornings, it is a dreadful thing for them to be effectively
divorced from the worship and preaching and teaching life of their

institutional churches. They may well be very sincere members of the church of Jesus Christ, the people of God, but without prayer and praise, without spiritual reflection together with other believers, they will be ill-informed, ill-developed, and often lonely Christians. Such laity are common enough now in many great city areas, struggling in a sincere, naive way to be Christians in their personal behavior, often trying to say some prayers, often hungry for a greater spiritual maturity, but basically quite ill-equipped to meet the tremendous challenges of their secular responsibilities. They lack both theological and spiritual skills.

If they lose a great deal by not being wholehearted participants in a Christian community and in a pattern of regular worship, the institutional churches also lose by being effectively out of touch with them. Both clergy and other laity need a living, friendly, controversial fellowship with their politically minded, aggressive fellow Christians. So often a parish becomes more and more a narrow fellowship of clergy and the "softer," idealistic laity, tends to recruit only that kind of people, and then half-proudly, half-guiltily labels the others "disloyal."

We must be very clear that a new and stronger church membership for "fringe" laity cannot be thought of as just a return to traditional patterns of suburban or country church life. We have still not taken seriously the words of that great pioneer in laity concerns, J. H. Oldham, when he wrote nearly thirty years ago:

> There is a great deal of talk in church circles at the present time about the importance of the laity. But the question is approached almost invariably from the wrong end. What is usually meant is that more laymen should come in and give their support to the Church as it is. That is just what a large number of the best laypeople standing on the fringe will not do. The much more important question to which the Church needs to address its mind is its own need of the experience which these people have of life, to widen its outlook and deepen its understanding, so that it may become a more effective force in society. If Christianity is not something existing apart from life, but the transfiguration of life itself—and that means in the end the transfiguration of the whole of life—it is those who are in the front line of the battle and are exposed to the severest tests who are best able to teach us what Christianity means as a living faith. It is through its lay members that the Church makes contact with the life of the world.[1]

Not More and More Church Jobs

Some clergy, and some conferences organized for laity, still assume that a major trade union official, or journalist, or corporation executive will be led by the Lord to return to the local church on the basis of undertaking leadership in a stewardship campaign, or on a committee for clergy pensions, or for a rebuilding fund, or similar maintenance programs. Yes, from time to time it may be right for busy and burdened Christians to do these things, either because there is an overwhelming parish crisis or because such relatively trivial matters (in terms of their secular responsibilities) may be almost a relaxation enjoyed with congenial companions and not their throat-cutting competitors. Nevertheless, at the risk of being very unpopular with some of my clergy friends, I must venture to suggest that many church jobs should be undertaken only on retirement from active participation in politics or business or other "front line" occupations. Even prestigious lay responsibilities like fund raising for a great cathedral or a major denominational cause can be a trap to deflect first-class laity from theologizing and working *in the world*. It is not an easy thing to face, but some otherwise admirable parishes have still to accept the fact that they must not expect laymen and laywomen actively involved in secular occupations to do minor maintenance jobs, any more than an army uses commando troops to run base areas. In fact it may be a test of the servanthood of many clergy and of many laity to accept such in-church jobs for themselves, and to praise God that in this way they can free others for witness in the world.

Obligations

Some laity, then, may properly plead other priorities in order to escape (but not in any superior attitude) some church duties and chores. What, however, are their inescapable obligations as church members?

1. All God's people, from the president to the poorest illiterate, have an obligation to worship regularly, even if not legalistically, every single Sunday; to pay something to make that worship possible; and to provide for an educated clergy and an adequate church

organization—with the proviso always that the people who pay have a right to know about and indeed a duty to question church budgets, which often automatically finance the same things that they did twenty or even fifty years ago. (I have never forgotten a former student of mine remarking, "Nothing is more spiritually enervating than to be expected to put your scarce energies and cash into buildings which you do not believe in.") I hold that even the busiest laity are not exempt from some kind of church attendance and support; I leave to one side the question as to what kind of worship they should attend. In fact the great variety of denominational worship and of informal and formal services gives us all far more choice, even within one denomination, than in the days before the automobile.

2. Christians with particular secular skills and responsibilities have a special opportunity to help in Christian education, both of teen-agers and of adults. I remember the fine witness of Dr. Edward Lindaman when he was a space scientist (which he has continued as president of Whitworth College). He refused to join in many of the club activities of his local church, but he was always prepared—together with his wife—to take a senior-high church class as often as he could. This was a fine example of a major rule in Christian formation and development: that the young learn most from the example and the explicit testimony of their parents and relatives and other adult *laity* whom they know. It may be that they will decide to become adult Christians themselves; it may be that they will, one way or another, either quietly or vociferously reject church membership (and maybe the gospel itself).

A young bank clerk learns a great deal about the faith (good or bad) from contact with a senior banker who is distinctively Christian. (What does such a person say about redlining, about South Africa, about minority employment problems? If the banker's superiors are unsympathetic, how does the banker survive?) Young people can be turned on or off about politics by helpful or unhelpful discussions with avowed Christian politicians far more than by earnest talks from either clergy or political science teachers. The "don't trust anybody over thirty" myth of the 1960s did a great deal to upset the traditional professional relationships between experienced practitioners and their apprentices, but things are becoming more normal now, with some gains on both sides.

In any case it is, I believe, an obligation of senior, veteran Christian politicians, lawyers, and other leaders to be available to their successors. If their offers of advice are spurned, that has often been so in professional relationships; but they can be much wiser and more effective "ministers" than any outsiders, be they laity or clergy. In particular (again it has been a special concern of Dr. Lindaman's), able laity may encourage younger Christians to look forward into the future, rather than to fall into the heresy of imagining that Christian theology is mostly a matter of past ages and historical loyalties and controversies.[2] This is not just a matter of looking forward with some Christian hope, it is also a style of thinking and planning ahead for personal careers, for genuinely new kinds of discipleship, for an adequate investment in the future. It was a delightful and unusual experience to hear a church administrator say, when it was time to choose delegates to a world conference, "The important thing is to consider who is going to be around in twenty years time." Most major denominations are quite dreadfully negligent in future planning for their clergy leadership, let alone for their laity. Lay people who spend a great deal of their time looking ahead, planning for their own retirement and for the next generation of experts and leaders, can help the church from being "dragged at the cartwheel of history," as Bishop Dibelius of Berlin used to say.

3. I believe that such laity can be extremely valuable in discerning the mind of Christ in all kinds of modern problems and opportunities. Not many major churches have developed the art of Christian "think tanks," where the special insights of particularly competent laity may be articulated, assessed, criticized, and then communicated to the general body of church members. (The work of the Church of England Board of Social Responsibility and Dr. Paul Abrecht's studies for the World Council of Churches are two conspicuous achievements in this way of doing things.) Far more often, a few such laity are incorporated into a *Committee for This* or a *Task Force Against That*, dominated by morally energetic but

rather uninformed clergy, who produce white-hot denunciations in such general terms that they are very little use. Even worse, busy laity are asked to help with a debate on ecology or energy or Iran, only to find that they have to spend several hours listening to church pension problems before such burning items on the Synod agenda are introduced. The designs of synods, conferences, and so on, need to be reconsidered, so that very occupied laity can come (maybe on Saturday or Sunday—yes, Sunday) to engage in really important debates. Maintenance and pension and churchly questions can be dealt with during an ordinary weekday.

How Can the Churches Help?

To worship, to help in church self-education, to help discern the mind of Christ for the denomination or the Council of Churches: these are the priority demands which may rightly be made of busy, overoccupied laity. What may such laity expect in return from their institutional churches?

Firstly, the laity may expect that the mission and ministry of the people of God in and through the secular structures of society be remembered constantly in prayer and in worship, and not, as often happens, be forgotten. Why should a new Sunday-school teacher or usher be (rightly) honored in worship, but the Monday morning or Saturday night activities of other members of the congregation go almost unmentioned? I still come across parish registers (those little boxes of three-by-five-inch index cards) which do not even indicate the jobs and political and other interests of the church's members. How, then, can the clergy and the worship committee (let us assume that there is such an enlightened body) design the praises and the prayers and the meditations of the church community? I have never forgotten the almost embarrassing thanks which I received after I had led, because of some emergency, a worship service in a village church in England. I had mentioned explicitly in the intercessions the local policeman, the storekeeper, and innkeeper. In my innocence I had assumed that such would be normal practice: it had in fact never occurred within living memory.

That comes first. The prayer and worshiping life of the body must reflect the whole work and life of that body, not just the admirable activities of the clergy and of a few parish workers. The second thing which the laity should demand from a great denomination, if not from their parish church, is a certain number of opportunities (preferably ecumenical ones) for advanced Christian learning and argument about the exact and minute particulars of their special occupations and activities. This is something far more than a twenty-minute discussion in a parish lounge about multinationals, or about urban renewal, or about South Africa. It is extraordinary how few opportunities for such self-education exist, even in areas where the countryside is littered with Christian conference centers and the like. I said recently in a discussion with a seminary professor that it seemed to me that there was not one center dedicated to advanced Christian laity education in his entire state. He replied, ''There is not one in the whole of New England.'' Well, I suspect that he was exaggerating, but it is quite extraordinary that there are literally hundreds of excellent facilities in the United States dedicated to the education and further education of the clergy (this is fine), hundreds more dedicated to furthering parish life, personal counseling, and family growth (and this is fine too) but only a handful of places where one can learn, in depth, about the ministry of Christian politicians, Christian university presidents, Christian investment brokers, or Christian labor leaders. How many local clergy feel it their duty to keep up-to-date about such places, so that they can encourage suitable laity to go to them?

This is not, I insist, an elitist argument in the bad sense that the personal and theological development of a bank president matters any more to the Lord than the development of anyone else. It is to say that the laity engaged in more secular activities don't get a fair chance for laity education, and that this is very bad for them and for the whole people of God. Some churches on the continent of Europe have done far better than this; the German Protestant churches not only have a fine and well-financed system of clergy and parish education, but *also* a whole series of academies and other nonparish education centers. Such centers, with or without special buildings, but at least with specially qualified staff, ought to be available in many more places in North America and in Britain.

A Partnership with Church Leaders

Finally, any really effective integration of the laity with secular power into the institutional churches will require a new style of partnership between them and church leaders—who are mostly, of course, bishops, senior clergy, and seminary professors. I have watched with keen interest the way in which a few bishops of my acquaintance, over the years, have developed a really lively, argumentative, growing friendship with some of the "stronger" and less "churchly" laity in their provinces and cities. More often, I have seen an easy politeness, a nervousness about "giving" (Shall I offend him and lose the check? Will that damned bishop try to touch me again?), a careful amiability in the club or at official banquets, but not a real partnership which honors and encourages competence and discipleship on both sides. Certainly, a Christian politician can encourage a bishop's discipleship when it goes flat, as well as vice versa. I dare to suggest that one of the most effective, as well as one of the most costly, ministries which leading laity and clergy can give to each other is, somehow, *to find time* to meet informally and in depth, not just in polite social courtesies, but in a quiet (and certainly unpublicized) searching after the Lord's will.

The churches will do well to think again about the warning of that strong Roman Catholic thinker and fighter for the laity, Yves Congar, when he wrote:

> Certain priests . . . practically never get near the sort of men who are fully engaged in the stern competition of the world. They would rather avoid them. They are in contact with some men and women (and children, of course) who belong in some degree to the world of the devout: much religion, not much men. The devout world makes a sort of halo round them which isolates them from the real world of men. They run the risk of never meeting any but people of their own religious world, people like themselves: whereas the real world is very different, very separate from our world, and is becoming increasingly so.[3]

To which we must add that competent women engaged in the "stern competition" of secular structures may find themselves just as isolated from church leaders as anyone else.

Yes, Prophecy from the Church

Then, *after* such careful dialogues, and after considering many other Christian voices and other, far less powerful people—the "decision sufferers" not the decision makers—the church must honor the call and the obligation to "prophesy," to speak out. This should almost always be a statement and a commitment by leading laity as well as by bishops and senior clergy. To refuse at critical times to be neutral and silent is not only a duty under the gospel, it is a service to the world at large, to the "poor," and to the "rich" as well.

One of the reasons why I am often sad about ill-informed, overblown "prophesying," either from the pulpit or from a church drafting committee, is that it depreciates the currency of Christian criticism. It destroys the credibility of Christian thinking. It loses the attention of both Christian and non-Christian leaders in politics and economics. But timely, well-informed, theologically sharp criticism about poverty, about the jails, about political or police or business or media corruption is an obligation on church leaders, and a service—even if a painful one—which lay people caught up in secular structures must learn to accept. (Indeed sometimes they will be grateful that outsiders can say awkward things which they cannot easily publicize themselves.) To quote J. Irwin Miller once more, and to acknowledge his admirable lay leadership in this as in so much else relating to the responsibilities of big business:

> The Church dare not evade its obligation to proclaim God's judg-ment over all human activity, even as it proclaims his mercy and forgiveness. . . .
>   The role of prophet is active, often disruptive and always painful, and it is thoroughly unpleasant to those on the receiving end of the preaching. I know this, because if the Church today were to do its full duty, I would be among those called to repent. As an employer, I can see I should have moved more swiftly during the last thirty years in respect to equal treatment of blacks, women and the nationals of other countries. I should have been prodded to accept responsibility for helping solve the worst problems in the communities in which we operate. The Church should have reminded me in convincing terms that my right to make a profit could not be asserted at a cost to the quality of life anywhere else.[4]

Such a readiness to accept criticism, and indeed to help form it, requires a strong and fair partnership between clergy and laity quite different from the polite but insidious estrangement between them in the past. Such a development of their mutual ministry, not only in personal and family and parish affairs but also in an understanding of the use and misuse of power in modern society, is urgently necessary if the church of Jesus Christ is to speak with holy impatience to the condition of men and women today.

TEN PRAYERS FOR POWERFUL LAITY

I HAVE no doubt at all that some of my friends and readers will smile a little at this modest collection of simple and familiar prayers. (One of them has already expressed great surprise, which I found a little distressing, that a worldly layman should trespass on the territory of holy spirituality.) Nevertheless, this series of *Laity Exchange Books* must try to be genuinely helpful to lay people, even if they seem a little unoriginal to specialists. It is my experience—surely confirmed by several public opinion polls—that many laymen and women are anxious to pray regularly about their secular occupations, are eager for some guidance, and are not always happy with the flavor and tone of many of the books of prayers which are to be found in religious bookstores.

So here are a few prayers, which may help. I make no apology for mixing contemporary prayers and some of the great petitions of English-speaking Christendom, for I do not think that mature Christian lay people will let themselves be trapped either in archaic museum religion or in transitory trendiness. I am absolutely convinced that no Christian life can be satisfactory without some time for prayer, for praise, and for reflection. I am distressed that so often the prayers and worship of the churches omit any careful consideration of the responsibilities of the laity in the Monday-through-Saturday world. I am not ashamed to hope that this book may help its readers not only to think hard, but also to pray with conviction and with understanding.

1

We are new men and women in Christ,
Members of his Body, the world Church,
Citizens of the Kingdom of God.
We are called
We are free
We are rich
We are sent
We are ministers, servants.
Lord help us to fulfill our ministries.

                                        Amen

2

Almighty and everlasting God,
By whose Spirit the whole body of the Church is governed and
    sanctified,
Receive our supplications and prayers which we offer before thee
    for all estates of men in thy holy Church,
That every member of the same, in his vocation and ministry may
    truly and godly serve thee,
Through our Lord and Saviour Jesus Christ.

                                        Amen

3

Dear Lord

Thank you that I am sometimes strong,
Help me when I am still weak.
Thank you that I am sometimes wise,
Help me when I am still foolish.
Thank you that I have sometimes done well,
Forgive me the times that I have failed you.
And teach me to serve you and your world
        With love and faith and truth
        With hope and grace and good humor.

                                        Amen

4

O God, who knowest us to be set in the midst of so many and
    great dangers,
        that by reason of the frailty of our nature we cannot
        always stand upright;
Grant to us such strength and protection,
      as may support us in all dangers,
      and carry us through all temptations;
          through Jesus Christ our Lord.

                                            Amen

5

Dear Lord, you have told us many times
That to be rich and comfortable may so easily lead to spiritual
    poverty,
And that you are at home with the poor and the homeless.
Help me to watch for the traps of affluence,
              the corruptions of wealth,
              the misuse of privilege,
So that I may still be loyal to you and the Gospel
Even in the temples of secular power,
Through Jesus Christ our Saviour.

                                            Amen

6

Lord, I do not ask
      for work equal to my strength
But for strength equal to your opportunities for me.

                                            Amen

7

Help me, Lord, to travel the miles for you
Efficiently and patiently and with some fun and style
Taking what rest and refreshment I can on the way
And content to travel home when this is possible.

Amen

8

O God the Creator and Preserver of all mankind
    we humbly beseech thee for all sorts and conditions of men;
That thou wouldest be pleased to make thy ways known unto them,
    thy saving health unto all nations.
More especially we pray for thy holy Church universal;
    That it may be so guided and governed by thy good Spirit,
        That all who profess and call themselves Christians
          May be led into the way of truth
          And hold the faith
            in unity of spirit,
            in the bond of peace,
            and in righteousness of life.
Finally we commend to thy fatherly goodness
        All those who are any ways afflicted, or distressed,
          in mind, body or estate
That it may please thee to comfort and relieve them, according to
    their several necessities;
      giving them patience under their sufferings,
      and a happy issue out of all their afflictions,
And this we beg for Jesus Christ's sake.

Amen

9

Dear God and Father of us all,
     Thank you for my calling in Jesus Christ,
     For my occupation and my work,
     For my family and friends.

Thank you for my gifts and strengths,
Forgive me for my sins and failures.

I know that today I must be very busy;
Help me also to be courteous and a good colleague.

Some decisions I may make,
Others I may have to suffer,
Others I may have to wait for,

Grant me a right judgment in these things.

Amen

10

O Lord support us all the day long of this troublous life,
Until the shadows lengthen and the evening comes
and the busy world is hushed and the fever of life is over
and our work is done.
Then Lord in thy mercy grant us a safe lodging, a holy rest, and
peace at the last.

Amen

Notes and Suggestions for Further Reading

THERE HAS BEEN in recent years a sad shortage of Christian writing on some *specialized* aspects of the life and witness of the laity (of course both the work of the Audenshaw Project and this present series of *Laity Exchange Books* are intended to make a contribution toward filling some of these gaps). I have therefore not hesitated to mention some thoughtful books of the 1950s and 1960s which, though in some ways out of date, still raise important questions about lay responsibilities.

1. A COMMON CALLING: SOME SPECIAL RESPONSIBILITIES

1. See *God's Frozen People* (Philadelphia: Westminster Press, 1965) and *God's Lively People* (Philadelphia: Westminster Press, 1971) for ways in which my colleague T. Ralph Morton and I developed these themes.

2. This remark was made in a conversation with Hugh Sykes Davies in the 1930s and is referred to in the *Times Literary Supplement,* 13 November 1970.

3. Barbara Brown Zikmund, "But I Have Called You Friends," an address before the 11th General Synod of the United Church of Christ, 2 July 1977, reprinted in *Laity Exchange* no. 3, March 1978.

4. Eugene Goodheart, *Culture and the Radical Conscience* (Cambridge, Mass.: Harvard University Press, 1973), p. 130.

5. In a very helpful paper, "Power and Powerlessness," prepared as part of the British Council of Churches Study, *Britain Today and Tomorrow* (1977), p. 1.

6. In a letter to the author, October 1974.

Suggestions for Further Reading:
The classic statements on the vocation of the laity are:

From the Protestant side:
Kraemer, Hendrik. *A Theology of the Laity.* Philadelphia: Westminster Press, 1959.

From the Roman Catholic side:
Congar, Yves. *Lay People in the Church: A Study for a Theology of the Laity.* Westminster, Md.: Newman Press, 1957.
The documents on the Apostolate of the laity and on the church:
Abbott, Walter M., ed. *The Documents of Vatican II.* New York: American Press and Association Press, 1966.

More popular books on the call to the laity and laity development are:
Bucy, Ralph, ed. *The New Laity between Church and World.* Waco, Tex.: Word Books, 1978. Contributors from *The Laity: A New Direction* group.
Butt, Howard, and Elliot, E. Wright. *At the Edge of Hope: Christian Laity in Paradox.* New York: Seabury Press, 1968.
Diehl, William E. *Christianity and Real Life.* Philadelphia: Fortress Press, 1976.
Greenleaf, Robert K. *Servant Leadership.* New York: Paulist Press, 1977. The definitive collection of his wise and influential essays.
Hall, Cameron P., ed. *Listening to Lay-People.* New York: Council Press, 1971.
———. *Lay-Action—The Church's Third Force.* New York: Friendship Press, 1974.
Stott, John R. W. *One People: Clergy and Laity in God's Church.* London: Falcon Books, 1968.
Vos, Nelson. *Monday's Ministries: The Ministry of the Laity.* Philadelphia: Parish Life Press, 1979. Strongly recommended.
Weber, Hans-Ruedi. *Salty Christians.* New York: Seabury Press, 1963.
Wentz, Frederick K. *The Layman's Role Today.* Garden City, N.Y.: Doubleday, 1963. A challenge to laymen to be Christians in their daily lives.
———. *Getting into the Act.* Nashville, Tenn.: Abingdon Press, 1978.
Russell, Bertrand. *Power: A Social Analysis.* New York: Norton, 1969. By far the most helpful general analysis of power in modern society.

2. THE STRAINS AND THE COMPROMISES

1. James McGregor Burns, *Leadership* (New York: Harper and Row, 1978). See especially parts 3 and 4.

2. Saul Alinsky, *Rules for Radicals* (New York: Vintage Books, 1972), p. 25.
3. See in particular Helmut Thielicke, *Theological Ethics,* vol. 2, *Politics,* part 3, "Borderline Situations" (Philadelphia: Fortress Press, 1969; repr. Grand Rapids, Mich.: William B. Eerdmans, 1979).
4. Philip Mason, *The Dove in Harness* (New York: Harper and Row, 1976), p. 23. Mr. Mason, a civil servant in India for many years, also writes under the name of Philip Woodruff.

Suggestions for Further Reading:
Mouw, Richard. *Political Evangelism.* Grand Rapids, Mich.: William B. Eerdmans, 1973.
Nader, Ralph; Petkas, Peters; and Blackwell, Kate, eds. *Whistle Blowing: The Report of the Conference on Professional Responsibility.* New York: Bantam Books, 1972.
Niebuhr, Reinhold. *Moral Man and Immoral Society: A Study in Ethics and Politics.* New York: Scribner, 1932.
Rose, Arnold M. *The Power Structure: Political Process in American Society.* New York: Oxford University Press, 1967.

3. UNDER BRUTAL STRAIN

1. See reports from Freedom House, 20 West 40th St., New York, NY 10018; from Amnesty International, Room 64, 200 West 72nd St., New York, NY 10023; and the excellent article by Robert Skelton, "The Geography of Disgrace, a World Survey of Political Prisoners," *Saturday Review,* 15 June 1974, p. 14.
2. Trevor Beeson, *Discretion and Valour: Religious Conditions in Russia and Europe* (London: Collins Fontana Books, 1974).
3. Werner Huhne, *A Man to Be Reckoned With: The Story of Reinold von Thadden-Trieglaff,* ed. Mark Gibbs (London: SCM Press, 1962); see especially chapters 4–7.
4. Martin Conway, *Audenshaw Papers* no. 71, p. 2.
5. John Colville, *Footprints in Time* (London: Collins, 1976), p. 277.

Suggestions for Further Reading:
The literature on prisons, concentrations camps and torture chambers in this century will be well-known to many readers. Here are just a few references:
Bonhoeffer, Dietrich. *Letters and Papers from Prison,* enl. ed. New York: Macmillan, 1972. A classic book of reflections on prison life, though until the last days he did not suffer extreme privation.

Cassidy, Sheila. *Audacity to Believe.* Cleveland: Collins, 1978.
Cristo, Carlos Alberto Libanio. *Against Principalities and Powers.*
Maryknoll, N.Y.: Orbis Books, 1977. Famous letters from a Brazilian
jail.
Koestler, Arthur. *Darkness at Noon.* New York: Bantam, 1979. His
marvelous novel about psychological interrogation.
Miller, Allen O. *A Christian Declaration on Human Rights.* Grand
Rapids, Mich.: William B. Eerdmans, 1977.
Solzhenitsyn Aleksandr I. *Gulag Archipelago,* 3 vols. New York: Harper
and Row, 1979.

4. HELP FROM THE LOCAL CHURCH

1. See *The Unchurched American* (Princeton, N.J.: Princeton Religion
Research Center, 1978).
2. See Theodore A. Eastman, "New Life in a Congregation,"
Audenshaw Papers no. 18 (Belford Presbyterian Church N.Y.), and
William B. Abernethy, *A New Look for Sunday Morning* (Nashville,
Tenn.: Abingdon Press, 1975) (South Congregational Church in Middle-
town, Conn.).
3. Max Warren, *The Day of the Preacher* (London: Mowbrays, 1967),
p. 43.
4. Urban T. Holmes, *Ministry and Imagination* (New York: Seabury
Press, 1976), p. 215.
5. James C. Fenhagen, *Mutual Ministry: New Vitality for the Local
Church* (New York: Seabury Press, 1977).
6. Gabriel Moran, *Vision and Tactics: Towards an Adult Church* (London: Burns and Oates, 1968) and *Design for Religion* (New York: Herder
and Herder, 1979).
7. Hans Küng, *On Being a Christian* (New York: Doubleday, 1976),
p. 522.
8. Basil Higginson, *Finding Time for Service, Item* no. 47, January
1966.

Suggestions for Further Reading:

Miller, John M. *The Contentious Community.* Philadelphia: Westminster
Press, 1979. On conflicts which disturb local congregations.
Moran, Gabriel, *Vision and Tactics: Towards an Adult Church.* London:
Burns and Oates, 1968.
Noyce, Gaylord B. *The Responsible Suburban Church.* Philadelphia:
Westminster Press, 1967.
Russell, Letty M. *Christian Education in Mission.* Philadelphia:
Westminster Press, 1967.

5. HELP OUTSIDE THE LOCAL PARISH

1. Mark Gibbs and T. Ralph Morton, *God's Lively People* (Philadelphia: Westminster Press, 1971).
2. See Don Smith, "A Style of Laity Seminars," *Audenshaw Documents* no. 29, p. 1.
3. Harold C. Letts, "Lutheran Support for Laity in the World," *Laity Exchange* no. 3 (March 1978).
4. E. Mollie Batten, "The Arguments Can Be Free and Frank: The Story of William Temple College," *Christian Comment* no. 76 (December 1966), p. 2.
5. Dr. de Lange is at present preparing a report on this work for a future issue of *Laity Exchange*.

Suggestions for Further Reading:

Many of the reports on specialist laity groups and centers outside local congregations are now a little dated except for recent books on Christian communes and fellowships, which do not always speak particularly to the problems of Christians with secular power. Two books on European laity centers that are still valuable are:

Frakes, Margaret. *Bridges to Understanding*. Philadelphia: Muhlenberg (now Fortress) Press, 1960.

Gable, J. Lee. *Church and World Encounter*. New York: United Church Press, 1964.

Four recent books are:

Diehl, William E. *Christianity and Real Life*. Philadelphia: Fortress Press, 1976.

Vos, Nelson. *Monday's Ministries*. Philadelphia: Parish Life Press, 1979.

Wentz, Frederick K. *Getting into the Act: Opening up Lay Ministry in the Weekday World*. Nashville, Tenn.: Abingdon Press, 1978.

Wren, Brian. *Education for Justice*. London: SCM Press, 1976.

The publication *Laity Exchange* (which is helping to sponsor this series, *Laity Exchange Books*) includes news of recent developments in non-parish work. Details may be obtained from Vesper Center, 311 MacArthur Boulevard, San Leandro, CA 94577.

6. CHRISTIAN POLITICIANS

1. See, for example, William Temple, *Christianity and Social Order* (London: SCM Press, 1942) and Reinhold Niebuhr, *Moral Man and Immoral Society* (New York: Scribner, 1932).
2. See, for example, *The New Face of Evangelicalism, an International*

Symposium on the Lausanne Covenant, ed. C. Rene Padilla (London: Hodder & Stoughton, 1976), especially chapter 5.

3. Richard Mouw has developed this theme in several books, including the first in this *Laity Exchange Books* series: *A Call to Holy Worldliness.*

4. Jacques Ellul, *The Betrayal of the West* (New York: Seabury Press, 1978), p. 89.

5. Irving L. Horowitz, *Ideology and Utopia in the United States 1956–1976* (New York: Oxford University Press, 1977), p. 192.

6. See, for example, Doris Kearns, *Lyndon Johnson and the American Dream* (New York: Harper and Row, 1976); especially chapter 8, "The Great Society."

7. See Stewart Alsop, *The Center* (New York: Popular Library, 1968); Charles L. Clapp, *The Congressman, His Work As He Sees It* (New York: Doubleday Anchor Books, 1964); Stimson Bullitt, *To Be a Politician* (New York: Doubleday Anchor Books, 1977), p. 13.

8. Jean Monnet, *Memoirs* (New York: Doubleday, 1978).

9. Mark Hatfield, *Between a Rock and a Hard Place* (New York: Pocket Books, 1977), p. 13.

10. Arthur Gish, *The New Left and Christian Radicalism* (Grand Rapids, Mich.: William B. Eerdmans, 1970), p. 95. I am grateful to Richard Mouw for reminding me of this important reference.

Suggestions for Further Reading:

Cotham, Perry. *Politics, Americanism and Christianity.* Grand Rapids, Mich.: Baker Book House, 1976. A strong evangelical comment.

Crozier, Michel. *The Bureaucratic Phenomenon.* Chicago: University of Chicago Press, 1964. A seminal work on bureaucracy.

Hatfield, Mark O. *Not Quite So Simple.* New York: Harper and Row, 1968.

Most of the books on John F. Kennedy, Lyndon Johnson, and Richard Nixon have insights on the pace and confusion and temptations of decision making at the higher levels of government.

7. CHRISTIAN BUSINESS EXECUTIVES

1. Irving Kristol, *Two Cheers for Capitalism* (New York: New American Library, 1979), p. 73.

2. Denys Munby, "The Two-Facing Role of the Businessman," *The Journal of Religion* (January 1959); reprinted in *God and the Rich Society* (New York: Oxford University Press, 1961), p. 198.

3. Abraham Zaleznik, "Power and Politics in Organizational Life," *Harvard Business Review*, May–June 1970, p. 48. See also Robert N. McMurry, "Power and the Ambitious Executive," *Harvard Business Review*, November–December 1973, p. 140.

4. J. Irwin Miller on CBS-TV, December 1967. Mr. Miller is chairman of the board of Cummings Engine Company, Inc., Columbus, Indiana, and a past president of the National Council of Churches.

5. C. Mills Wright, *The Power Elite* (New York: Oxford University Press, 1956), p. 343; see especially chapter 15, "The Higher Immorality."

6. Irving Kristol, "Ethics and the Corporation," *The Wall Street Journal*, 16 April 1975.

7. Brian Wren, *Education for Justice* (New York: Orbis Books, 1977); William Coats, *God in Public: Political Theology beyond Niebuhr* (Grand Rapids, Mich.: William B. Eerdmans, 1974).

8. The conference was held at the Massachusetts Institute of Technology, Cambridge, Mass. in July 1979. This section report, Restructuring the Industrial and Urban Environment, is included in *Faith and Science in an Unjust World*, vol. 2 (Philadelphia: Fortress Press, 1980).

9. See the report on this work by Martin Stäbler in *Laity Exchange* no. 3.

10. In an important article, "The Future of the Multinational," *Worldview*, November 1976, p. 4.

11. "The International Corporation: an Executive's View," *The Annals of the American Academy*, Fall 1972, p. 21.

Suggestions for Further Reading:

Bowen, Howard R. *Social Responsibilities of the Businessman.* New York: Harper and Bros., 1953.

Childs, Marquis W. and Cater, Douglass. *Ethics in a Business Society.* New York: Harper and Bros., 1954.

Both these older books are well worth reading, and reflect responsible "liberal" opinion of the times.

Diehl, William E. *Christianity and Real Life.* Philadelphia: Fortress Press, 1976. See especially his reflections as sales manager of a major steel corporation.

Nankivell, Owen. *All Good Gifts.* London: Epworth Press, 1978.

Preston, Ronald H. *Religion and the Persistence of Capitalism.* Naperville, Ill.: Allenson, 1979. Serious and important lectures on Christian faith and economic affairs.

Silk, Leonard and Vogel, David. *Ethics and Profits: The Crisis of Confidence in American Business.* New York: Simon and Schuster, 1976.

Vernon, Raymond. *Storm over the Multinationals: The Real Issues.* Cambridge, Mass.: Harvard University Press, 1977.

8. CHRISTIAN LABOR UNION LEADERS

1. Jerome Davis, *Labour Speaks for Itself on Religion* (New York: Macmillan, 1929).
2. Davis, *Labour Speaks for Itself on Religion,* p. 131.
3. John A. Fitch, *The Social Responsibilities of Organized Labor* (New York: Harper and Bros., 1957).
4. See William Kornblum, *Blue Collar Community* (Chicago: University of Chicago Press, 1974).
5. Steven Brill, *The Teamsters* (New York: Simon & Schuster, 1978).
6. D. C. Bok and J. T. Dunlop, eds., *Labor and the American Community* (New York: Rockefeller Brothers Fund, 1979).
7. J. B. S. Hardman, *Labor at the Rubicon* (New York: New York University Press, 1972).
8. A. H. Raskin, "The Big Squeeze on Labor Unions," *Atlantic,* October 1978, p. 41.
9. Clive Jenkins and Barrie Sherman, *The Collapse of Work* (London: Eyre-Methuen, 1979).
10. A. H. Raskin, "Big Labor Strives to Break out of Its Rut," *Fortune,* 27 August 1979, p. 41.
11. Kornblum, *Blue Collar Community;* Robert Schrank, *Ten Thousand Working Days* (Cambridge, Mass.: MIT Press, 1978).
12. Kornblum, *Blue Collar Community,* p. 185.
13. Patrick J. Sullivan, "The Churches and the Union," *America,* 9 June 1979, p. 473.
14. George G. Higgins, "Born Again Coalition? A Modest Beginning," *Commonweal,* 22 June 1979, p. 356.
15. Cameron P. Hall, "Towards a More Humane Society," *Engage/ Social Action,* April 1973, p. 31.
16. Cameron P. Hall, *Lay Action—The Church's Third Force* (New York: Friendship Press, 1974), p. 52.

Suggestions for Further Reading:

Betten, Neil B. *Catholic Activism and the Industrial Worker.* Gainesville, Fla.: University Presses of Florida, 1976. A bibliographic study.
Dutton, Frederick G. *The Changing Sources of Power.* New York: McGraw Hill, 1972. Has an important section (pp. 141 ff.) on labor unions today.

Rosow, Jerome M. *The Worker and the Job: Coping with Change.* New York: Prentice Hall, 1974.

9. CHRISTIAN LEADERS IN THE POLICE AND THE MILITARY

1. See Albert J. Reiss, Jr., *The Police and the Public* (New Haven, Conn.: Yale University Press, 1971), especially chapter 4.
2. James F. Ahern, *Police in Trouble* (New York: Hawthorn Books, 1972), p. 103.
3. Ahern, *Police in Trouble,* p. 196.
4. John Kenneth Galbraith, *How to Control the Military* (New York: Signet Books, 1969), pp. 26–27.
5. Lewis H. Lapham, "Military Theology," *Harper's Magazine,* July 1971, pp. 73–85.
6. Galbraith, *How to Control the Military,* p. 75.
7. Peter L. Berger, "Reflections on Patriotism," *Worldview,* July 1974, pp. 19–25.
8. John Le Carré, *The Spy Who Came In from the Cold* (New York: Bantam Books, 1973); *Smiley's People* (New York: Knopf, 1980).

Suggestions for Further Reading:

Bennett, John C. and Seifert, Harvey. *U. S. Foreign Policy and Christian Ethics.* Philadelphia: Westminster Press, 1977. A critical but not extreme position on foreign policy and military actions.
Church Information Office. *Police: A Social Study.* London: Church Information Office, 1967.
Ellul, Jacques. *The Technological Society.* New York: Knopf, 1964. For a pessimistic view on police control in the future see pp. 101 ff.
Enz, Jacob J. *The Christian and Warfare.* Scottsdale, Pa.: Herald Press, 1972. A biblical pacifist position, with roots in the Old Testament.
Kahn, Herman and Bruce-Briggs, B. *Things to Come: Thinking about the Seventies and Eighties.* New York: Macmillan, 1972. On the politicization of the police.
Morganthau, Hans J. *Truth and Power.* New York: Praeger, 1970. Chapter 27 is important to the police in their political setting.
Royko, Mike. *Boss: Richard J. Daley of Chicago.* New York: Signet Books, 1971. An important section on Chicago police, pp. 110 ff.
Walzer, Michael. *Just and Unjust Wars.* New York: Basic Books, 1979.
Yarmolinsky, Adam and Lambert, Richard D., ed. *The Military and American Society.* Annals of American Academy of Political and Social Science, no. 406 (1973).

10. CHRISTIANS AND THE POWER OF THE MEDIA

1. Malcolm Muggeridge, *Christ and the Media* (Grand Rapids, Mich.: William B. Eerdmans, 1978).

2. Jerry Mander, *Four Arguments for the Elimination of Television* (New York: William Morrow, 1978).

3. Erik Barnouw, *The Sponsor: Notes on a Modern Potentate* (New York: Oxford University Press, 1978).

4. Albert van den Heuvel, *Theology, Communication and the Mass Media*. A mediation published by the Broadcasting Divisions of the Anglican, Roman Catholic, and United Churches of Canada, 1968.

5. Carll Tucker, "Our Curious Business," *Saturday Review,* 12 November 1977, p. 14.

6. Byron Shafer and Richard Larson, "Did TV Create the 'Social Issue'?" *Columbia Journalism Review,* September 1972, p. 10.

7. J. William Fulbright, "On the Press," *Columbia Journalism Review,* November–December 1975, p. 42.

8. Jack Richardson, "Six O'Clock Prayers: TV News as Pop Religion," *Harpers Magazine,* December 1975, p. 34.

9. Leonard Woolf, *Downhill all the Way* (New York: Harcourt Brace Jovanovich, 1967), p. 140.

10. World Association of Christian Communication, 122 Kings Road, London, S.W.3, England.

11. Michael J. Arlen, *The View from Highway 1* (New York: Farrar, Strauss & Giroux, 1976); Nicholas Johnson, *How to Talk Back to Your Television Set* (Boston: Little Brown, 1970); Reports on Television Awareness Training from MARC, 475 Riverside Drive, Suite 1370, New York, NY 10027.

Suggestions for Further Reading:

Adler, Ruth, ed. *The Working Press.* New York: Bantam Books, 1970. *New York Times* reporters on their work.

Bluck, John. *Beyond Neutrality: A Christian Critique of the Media.* Geneva: World Council of Churches, 1978.

Priestland, Gerald. *The Dilemmas of Journalism.* London: Lutterworth Press, 1979.

11. POWERFUL LAITY AND THE INSTITUTIONAL CHURCHES

1. Joseph H. Oldham, *Life Is Commitment* (London: SCM Press, 1953), p. 86.

2. Edward B. Lindaman, *Thinking in the Future Tense* (Nashville, Tenn.: Broadman Press, 1978).

3. Yves Congar, *Priest and Layman* (London: Darton, Longman and Todd, 1967), p. 254.
4. Irwin J. Miller, "Should Churches 'Play It Safe'?" *Presbyterian Life,* May 1972, p. 48.

Suggestions for Further Reading:

Baum, Gregory. *The Social Imperative.* New York: Paulist Press, 1979.

Equality and Justice for All. Christian Calling in an Age of Interdependence. New York: Lutheran Church in America, 1976. Study by the Division for Mission in North America.

Hess, H. Ober, ed. *The Nature of a Humane Society.* Philadelphia: Fortress Press, 1977. Theological reflections mixed in with comments from politicians, scientists, and others.

Illich, Ivan D. *Celebration of Awareness.* Garden City, N.Y.: Doubleday, 1970. A call for institutional awareness.

Linzen, Jorge. *The Politics of Altruism.* Geneva: Lutheran World Federation, 1977. The political involvement of church and other voluntary development agencies.

TEN PRAYERS FOR POWERFUL LAITY

Prayers 4 and 8 are from the English *Book of Common Prayer,* 4 is the Collect for the Fourth Sunday after the Epiphany, 8, A Prayer for All Conditions of Men. Prayer 2 is from *Each Returning Day* (London: BBC Publications, 1940), p. 21. Prayer 10 is a sixteenth-century prayer from Cecil Hunt, *Uncommon Prayers* (London: Hodder & Stoughton, 1963), p. 60. The rest are anonymous.